Goldwin Smith

The Civil War in America

An address read at the last meeting of the Manchester Union and

Emancipation Society

Goldwin Smith

The Civil War in America
An address read at the last meeting of the Manchester Union and Emancipation Society

ISBN/EAN: 9783337410735

Printed in Europe, USA, Canada, Australia, Japan

Cover: Foto ©ninafisch / pixelio.de

More available books at **www.hansebooks.com**

THE CIVIL WAR IN AMERICA:

AN ADDRESS

READ AT THE LAST MEETING OF THE MANCHESTER
UNION AND EMANCIPATION SOCIETY.

BY

GOLDWIN SMITH.

LONDON:

SIMPKIN, MARSHALL, & CO., STATIONERS' HALL COURT.

MANCHESTER: A. IRELAND & CO.

—

1866.

THE CIVIL WAR IN AMERICA.

THE civil war in America is over; the armies have gone home; the passions have subsided; and though the ashes still glow, though the time when an impartial history can be written has not arrived, we may try to understand the real import of the conflict—the real significance of the victory—and to read, as far as mortal eyes may read, the counsels of Providence in this the great event of our age.

This great struggle, like most of the great struggles in history, was complex in its character. In some measure its character changed as it went on. On the Southern side most were fighting for Slavery, but some for State Right. On the Northern side some were fighting against Slavery, but many were fighting for the Union. At the North the Anti-Slavery sentiment grew more predominant towards the close, both because the moral feeling of the people had been stirred and elevated by the struggle, and because they saw more clearly that Slavery was the root of the political evil, and a root from which, unless it was plucked up, the same evil would always grow. At first the majority would have compromised with Slavery for the sake of the Union, the source, as they deemed it, of their greatest blessings, the object of their fondest and most hallowed associations. If there is a nation which would readily

B

consent to disruption for a moral object, let it cast the first
stone at them for their weakness. But at the last Presi-
dential election, the question being distinctly put to the
people whether they would compromise with Slavery for
the Union, the people answered by a great majority that
they would not. Then the victory was given into their
hands. Let the nation which can boast of virtue pure
and unalloyed, which has needed no pressure of circumstances to force it into the right way, no suffering to purge
its vision that it might clearly discern good from evil, no
chastisement to teach it the will of Heaven—let this
nation, I say again, cast the first stone. To the American
people the Union was not empire only, but immunity
from hostile neighbourhood and standing armies ; it was
the pledge not of power only, but of liberty and peace.

That Slavery was the cause of the war, who can sincerely doubt ? Secession broke out and had its focus in
the centre of Slavery, spread wherever Slavery prevailed,
was most intense where Slavery prevailed most. It did not
extend to the free districts of the South, Western Virginia
and Eastern Tennessee, the inhabitants of which were
dragged into the Confederacy by force. It exactly followed
the wavering line of slavery in the mixed States, Maryland,
Kentucky, and Missouri. The secession ordinances proclaimed as the ground, and the sole ground, of the revolt
the rights of Slavery, threatened by Northern abolition.
The Southern prophets all prophesied of a vast slave empire as the reward of success. Visions of such an empire,
stretching from the grave of Washington to the hills of
Montezuma, filled the minds of Secessionists, as visions of
a perfect Christian society and of a reign of Christ on earth
filled the minds of the Wycliffites and the Puritans, as

visions of a Brotherhood of Man filled the minds of enthu-
siasts on the eve of the French Revolution. On the other
hand, the Anti-Slavery sentiment was called forth at the
North as strongly as the Pro-Slavery sentiment at the
South. And the immediate result of the victory has been
the downfall of Slavery, not in the United States only,
but everywhere and for ever.

The theory that the war arose from a divergence of
commercial interest, that it was a struggle between free
trade producers on one side and protectionist manufacturers on the other, though skilfully devised for
the market of English opinion, was defective in two
respects. It did not fit the facts, and the cause it
assigned was inadequate to produce the effect. It did
not fit the facts ; for the Western States were producers as well as the Southern, and the Western States,
notwithstanding the predictions of their imminent secession, were as true as the New England States to the
Union, and as staunch for the war. The cause which it
assigned was inadequate to produce the effect, for when
did a mere divergence of commercial interest rend political
bonds so powerful, or lead to such a civil war ? It is too
true that the manufacturers and ironmasters of the North
are still in the gall of Protection, that they still resist
those economical laws of Providence in the observance of
which other nations are blessed, and that for them now, as
formerly for our protectionists, writers are found to veil
barbarous cupidity in the language of patriotism and
science. The same tendency is seen in our colonies, and
ignorance is its chief root. Perhaps this quarrel between
manufacturer and producer may have contributed to the
disruption as a secondary cause, but it was as a secondary

cause only. No mention was made of it in the manifestos of the seceding states.

The struggle was one between Freedom and Slavery. But it was something deeper than this. It was a struggle between Christianity and all that is most hostile to Christianity. Christianity had founded a great community in the New World. Slavery came up against that community, as Mahometanism, with its polygamy, its fatalism, its exterminating ferocity, came up against European Christendom ten centuries ago; and, like Mahometanism, it has been overthrown. The Powers of Good and Evil, in forms perhaps more sharply defined than they had worn in any previous encounter, have fought for that New World, and the Power of Good has conquered.

I went to the United States believing, I returned firmly convinced, that not democracy in America, but free Christianity in America, was the real key to the study of the people and their institutions. Democracy is a political arrangement, dealing, like all political arrangements, with the shallower interests of man. It would be reversing the order of causation to deduce from it the deeper parts of the character of the people.

I mean by Christianity nothing sectarian or narrow. I mean by it the spirit of Christian society—the spirit which has hitherto alone shown itself capable of animating and sustaining a real community; for the spurious communities of heathen antiquity were oligarchial communities of masters tyrannising over a people of slaves. I mean the spirit which is present in many a champion of humanity, who, since Christianity has been degraded by superstition and allied with social injustice, would scarcely call himself by the Christian name, but who is nevertheless

doing his part to convert the kingdoms of the world into
the kingdom of Christ; while others are labouring with
all their power, political and ecclesiastical, to retard that
conversion, though they may arrogate the name of Christian to themselves alone. I mean the spirit of faith in
God and man, of charity between man and man, of hope
for the future of humanity. I mean the spirit of progress
of which Christian hope is the life, and which, look where
you will, is confined to the nations of Christendom. I
mean the spirit of Christianity, not the mere form, dog-
matic, ceremonial, or ecclesiastical. Such Christianity
may be a nullity in sectarian theology. It is the great
reality of history.

In Europe Christianity is paralysed by the divisions of
the national Churches, each with a state creed imposed
by political power and maintained by the state clergy,
who are legally bound over against conviction, so that till
State and Church shall have been separated the divisions
of Christendom are hopeless. The Church in the Old
World is unable to do or attempt what it was intended to
do for man But two centuries ago, England, then in her
noblest mood—for never, in spite of her trade, her victories,
and her empire, has she been so noble as she was in the
days of Hampden, Falkland, Milton, and Cromwell—sent
forth a religious colony, which founded the great community of the New World. It was well chosen for its
high purpose that germ of English religion, law, and freedom. It was well chosen, and so was the place where it
was planted—a vast expanse divided by no strong natural
boundaries, and commercially united in all directions by the
courses of great rivers, so that national divisions, with the
political enmities and religious schisms which they entail,

could scarcely find a place ; while it was severed from the Old World by an ocean which steam has now narrowed, but which was broad enough at first to emancipate the New World from old influences, and give human progress a fresh spring.

By the same exodus, which brought Christianity out of the State Churches, society escaped from feudalism into a system founded on equality and justice. This social transition Europe for two centuries of abortive revolution has been striving in vain to effect. The feudal aristocracy has in some countries been overthrown ; but from the inability of untrained communities, with dangerous masses of destitution and with no moral stay stronger than that of a state religion, to carry on self-government, the nations have escaped from aristocracy only to become the prey of despotism, supported by great standing armies, which now arrests the progress of humanity here, and from which there is at present no visible escape, though we may be sure that God, who has not made the world for standing armies and their masters, will in time find a way.

The Western States of America are a colony of New England. The original company of pilgrims is the seed from which the whole tree has grown. No creative monad, imagined by science, could be more pregnant with a new order of things than that little band of exiles ; no moment in history is more solemn or more big with consequences than that in which the colony on its arrival in the New World made a set of laws for itself—laws for self-government—rational, unfeudal laws.

The little Puritan settlement is lost in a great nation, and the narrow Puritan religion has expanded, or is fast expanding, into something more comprehensive, though

still you trace the original type in all the lineaments of
the now mighty frame. But the Northern States remain
what their Puritan founders desired that they should ever
be, a plantation religious. In America two things must
strike every traveller, the equality of the habitations and
the number of places of worship. Not only in New
England is each city, each little town crowned with a
cluster of steeples, it is the same in the Far West; and
while Christianity is proclaimed to be dying here, its
churches are rising, built by free will, in apparently un-
hesitating faith, wherever the pioneer axe makes room in
the woods of Michigan, wherever the plough turns the soil
in the prairies of Illinois, on the distant hills of Iowa,
beneath the lonely headlands of the Upper Mississippi.
Men go to write the life of Christ beside the sepulchre
were he was laid; if they would go where Christianity is
spreading over the untrodden West, they might know the
meaning of the words, "He is risen indeed." There is every
outward sign of regard for religion among this people.
The churches are well filled, and Sunday is well kept.
Much of this perhaps may be deference to opinion; but
opinion itself is free. The government must study the
national character, and it always speaks as to a religious
nation.

In America, too, there is a cry of the decay of faith;
and there, too, less might be said of the decay of faith, if,
in the first place, faith were not confounded with a belief
in tradition; and if, in the second place, there were more
of charity, and more of hope. There is, however, a religious crisis there as well as here, though it is less severe
there than here; because in America there is no State
Church to bar with a solid obstruction the current of

religious thought, and chafe it into destructive fury. The doubts and perplexities which we are at this time called upon to meet manfully in reliance on the God of truth, Americans also are called upon to meet in the same spirit. In both countries some, unable to endure suspense, unable to watch the one hour, have lost their faith in Providence, and committed religious suicide, by casting themselves into the superstitions of the past. But there are two things going on at present in American Christendom widely different from the decay of faith, which may easily be taken for it. The first is the decline of clerical authority; the second is the breaking up of sectarian dogma, and the consequent approach of a reconciliation of the churches.

The decline of clerical authority in itself indicates no decrease of religious feeling among the people. It may indicate the reverse. Intellectually and spiritually, the pastor of a Puritan congregation stood far above his flock, who looked up to him as their half-inspired and almost infallible guide. Now the flock are more nearly on a level both intellectually and spiritually with their pastor, and can regard him as an infallible guide no more. The circumstances of Christian Churches, like those of other communities change, and their organisation must adapt itself to their circumstances. This holds good of all except the Roman Catholic clergy, whose authority purports to be founded on the supernatural powers of a divine order, not on the natural influence of character or mind, But the Roman Catholic clergy lose their flocks when the Irish have become educated, that is in the second or third generation.

The Churches of America, in the main, are offsets of the Churches of Europe. The New World has not yet had leisure to produce a theology of its own. There are the different Protestant sects, the Presbyterians, the Baptists, the Methodists, which three communions embrace the bulk of the people ; Presbyterianism being the religion of the section corresponding to our upper middle class, while the other two are the religions of the masses. There is Unitarianism, the religion of the cultivated, rather negative, it is said, in many cases, and tending to scepticism : not seldom, perhaps, a decent name which scepticism itself assumes among a religious people. There is Roman Catholicism, the religion of the Irish emigrants, and for them, in their uneducated state, indispensable ; somewhat more rational, less given to miracles, relics, and mariolatry, and, if the court of Rome would let it be, less intriguing than in Europe, but everywhere, it is to be feared, inherently anti-social and the inveterate enemy of united education. There is Anglicanism, the genteel religion of the rich and fashionable world, a character which it has kept since the colonial days, with an element of Romanism in it as here, and a clergy who, like ours, would fain be a priesthood, but with a democratic and lay ascendancy in its government which keeps these tendencies within bounds, while, in deference to the sentiment of a rational and charitable community, it ceases to utter the denunciatory dogmatism of the Athanasian Creed. Universalism, of which English divines speak with terror as a vast and portentous heresy, is simply Protestantism, less the more cruel doctrines of Calvinism, against which it is a reaction. The hardness and the tyranny of extreme Calvinism send not a few converts in America to Episcopacy itself. There are sects of a more enthusiastic and grotesque kind, such as life in the wilderness produces when religious passion is under no intellectual control. There is Cameronianism,

in its ancient sternness, resolutely and to its singular
honour excluding the slave-owner from its pale. The
Church of the Mormons is chiefly fed from the Old World.
Mormonism is in fact the English or Welsh peasant's
craving for a more equal lot, combined with his Old Testa-
ment fallacies and his wild apocalyptic faith. Materialism,
it is said, is found among the German emigrants, and
among them alone.

All the Churches must be and visibly are affected
by the element of political democracy which surrounds
them, and this not only in their forms of government but
even in their modes of thought. It is hard to believe in
an arbitrary God when all the institutions of man around
you preach justice. It is hard to believe in an unmerciful
God, when all the institutions of man around you preach
mercy.

If, however, America has produced no new theology
she has produced Religious Liberty; and from Religious
Liberty in time better things still will spring. The circumstances under which these waifs of all the Churches of
Christendom were cast upon the American coast were such
as to preclude the existence of a dominant sect and to for-
bid mutual persecution. For a moment the Calvinists of
New England displayed the intolerance which they had
learnt in the old world; but that moment was soon past.
The tendency of the British dominion to establish Anglicanism at the South ended with the dominion itself. Even
Roman Catholicism, in its turn a fugitive from persecution,
proclaimed toleration in its new abode. Not only the political and social equality, but the political and social union of
the Churches is almost complete, saving in the case of
Roman Catholicism; and even a Roman Catholic priest is

obliged to conform in some measure to the principles of a
society intolerant of intolerance alone, and to take part in
works of Christian benevolence with the clergy of other
creeds. Under the influence of political and social union,
ecclesiastical divisions are gradually giving way. Christian
character is brought into the foreground, sectarian dogma
is thrown into the background. The Churches are gradually falling, but through their ruins appear again the
lineaments of the Universal Church. Intolerant orthodoxy
still holds its ground in the heart of many Roman Catholics,
Anglicans, Calvinists; but it is on the defensive, and its
ramparts are tumbling down. In each sect there appears a
liberal party, suspected by the narrowly orthodox, and
tending to fusion with other churches. The same, when
the time comes, will be the process of reconciliation in the
Old World: Christians will not be be brought over by
controversy; but, when perfect religious liberty reigns,
they will be re-united by fellowship. In America at present
lies the best hope of the reconciliation of Christendom.
And where the best hope of its reconciliation lies, there
lies the best hope of the propagation of its faith.   India
has not been converted from Rome or Canterbury; perhaps
she may be converted from San Francisco.

When dogma is gone a rational theology will rise.   It
was well that America could not have a theology when
theology would have ministered to sectarian dogmatism.
It was well that she could not have a church art and a
ritual, while church art and ritual would have ministered
to superstition.

It is in the West, perhaps, that the religious mind
is most free, that sectarian dogma has least power, that
Christianity has most gone out of the churches which had

been its temples, and threatened to become its graves, into
the general life of the community at large. Yet the West,
I believe, is not irreligious. One Western man, at all
events, raised from a low estate to the dizziest elevation,
and there set to contend with appalling perils, was kept
calm and wise by his strong sense of the constant presence and the over-ruling providence of God. If I am
not misinformed, there is a great craving among the
Western people for theological truth of a certain kind.
Talk to them of the questions that come before our
Ecclesiastical Courts and they will probably pay you little
attention : but if you have anything to say in singleness
of purpose about the great and vital truths of religion,
there, if I mistake not, are the ears that will hear and the
hearts that will understand you.

Christianity, as the religion of light, has always—
always at least where her own light has not been turned
to darkness—preached and practised the duty of education.
The Reformers, appealing from tradition to individual
reason and conscience, and to the Written Word, were great
revivers of this duty. Of popular education, in fact, they
may be said to have been the founders ; for the edu-
cational charity of the middle ages was, for the most part,
practically confined to poor children destined for the
clerical order. The common school in America is the
offspring of the Puritan church. To adapt it to a society
of various creeds it has been in a certain sense secularised,
but it still retains a religious character, as do the motives
which support it, and is a bond not only of social and
political but of Christian union in the nation. There are,
I doubt not, great local inequalities and grave general
defects in American education. In the higher education

unquestionably there are grave defects, arising partly from
the excess of the democratic spirit, which will not suffer
academical authority to be exercised to the needful extent,
and lavishes literary and scientific degrees through un-
qualified institutions, which afford no security for the
proper tests. But America is the land in which the duty
of educating the people has been most distinctly recognised, and most universally performed ; in which, let me
add, that duty has been performed most for its own sake,
and least with the object of training children up in allegiance to any political or ecclesiastical system. And the
nation receives its reward in high political intelligence
pervading the whole people, and in industry which is the
source of doubled wealth, because it is not only active but
skilful, and not only skilful but inventive. The Patent
Museum, at Washington, bears striking testimony to the
inventiveness of American industry. The mansion of the
President, at Washington, has now twice borne striking
testimony to the political intelligence by which the whole
people is pervaded, and which can, of a farmer or mechanic,
make a ruler, the peer of those who were born to rule.

The first Christian society had all things in common.
So for a time had the Puritan settlement in New England.
This was in each case a primitive state destined soon to
give way to the exigencies of existing civilisation. But
perhaps before the final consummation of Christian history
that primitive state may again be virtually realised, not
by violence or sudden revolution, but through the gradual
operation of Christian influences, which, whenever they
decisively prevail, without taking away the landmarks of
property, transmute proprietorship into duty. Possibly the
communistic aspirations which break forth whenever the

soul of Christian society is deeply moved may not, after all, be pure chimeras, but only chimerical anticipations of a result as yet indefinitely distant. Be this as it may, Christianity, if it does not absolutely exact, does certainly love as fair a distribution as may be of this world's goods among those who are equal members of the Christian brotherhood. She abhors at least the hideous extremes of wealth and destitution. She abhors the sight of sumptuous palaces tenanted by Christians, with other Christians starving at their gates. The soul in truth is not so independent of the body that Christian aspirations and Christian excellence can easily exist where the whole being of great masses of the people is absorbed in the grim struggle with hunger. A very large proportion of crime is the offspring of want, and can be practically removed only by giving bread to the people. And how great an obstacle to Christianity are the feelings produced in the hearts of multitudes by the daily pressure of an unjust lot ! How many evil tempers against which Christian ministers preach are inevitably aggravated by institutions which the preachers think it their political duty to support ! In the United States the distribution of worldly goods is probably more equal, and the means of a decent livelihood are more assured to all than in any other country. Poverty, saving among the newly arrived emigrants, is rare ; want of bread almost unknown, except as the consequence of vice. There are no workhouses full of penal paupers, nor multitudes of labourers outside the workhouses living with penal pauperism always in view. The inmates of the public almshouses, even in the great cities, are few in number, and, for the most part, as I was told, not Americans by birth ; nor has American society been scared by the terrible cancer of

indigence into treating destitution as half a crime. The
houses seem those of one vast middle class. Nowhere do
you see palaces ; and, generally speaking, the eye of the
European visitor looks around in vain for the hovels of the
poor. The quarters of the Irish and German emigrants
in the great seaboard cities (especially those of the Irish,
who linger in their helplessness where they land) were the
only haunts of misery and squalor that met my eye. I
saw nothing so bad as the low quarters of Liverpool or of
London in the cities ; nothing approaching to the cabins of
the English, much less to those of the Irish peasantry in
the country. This is partly due to the bounty of nature
in a rich and virgin land, which helps to solve so many
difficulties in America, as, in justice to European legisla-
tors, we must always bear in mind. But it is also partly
the effect of just laws. In the transit to the new world
primogeniture and entail were left behind.

In England, the place of the old English yeoman knows
him no more. In his stead the great proprietor reigns.
But in the prairies of Illinois is a tract of deep rich soil,
stretching for hundreds of miles each way in one vast
plain, with only slight swells of undulation and without a
stone for the plough to strike against—an ocean of corn-
land, monotonous to the eye, yet redeemed from dreariness
by its glorious fruitfulness, which seems to bid all that
hunger in the earth come there and be fed. Through the
midst of it runs the railway, bringing down for the first
time all the implements and resources of scientific agriculture into the virgin wilderness, and, like the Nile in its
course through Egypt, turning everything round it into
fertility and wealth. From the handling of those harvests
stately cities have risen where forty years ago the Indian

wigwams stood. There the English yeoman has found his home again. There he once more tills his own land, often broad lands, and once more lives frank and free among his peers. The dry American air has made his once burly frame more spare and sinewy : enterprise and education have developed his forehead, and lent keenness to his eye. But he still retains his solid English virtues, his kindliness, his good sense, his reverence for the law, and to judge by the Sunday aspect of his villages, his fear of God. He is still formidable to his foes under Grant and Sherman, as he was when he drew the bow with Edward and the Black Prince. Still, too, he loves his country, restless and ever moving westward though he be. Boys did the work of men in Illinois while her brave husbandmen were gone by thousands and tens of thousands to the war : and by the side of her villages is many a grave tenanted by the slain, brought from distant battle fields to protest against the calumny that hirelings only fought for the government of the people. It is a good thing to go to Greece and Italy and to look with grateful reverence on the monuments of the illustrious past : and it is a good thing also to go to Illinois and see the blessing of heaven resting on the future. No doubt this prosperity depends on the abundance of unoccupied and fertile land ; and even that exhaustless store must some day be exhausted : but by that time perhaps great problems will have been solved.

A popular novelist, from whose unauthentic page Englishmen I suspect draw many of their notions of America, has represented the Americans as not honouring labour. If they do not, they are not good Christians ; for Christianity bids all its professors work if they would eat, forbidding any man to live in mere uselessness by the labour of his fellow. But here, as in many other cases, as in the stories of duelling and stabbing, what was true only of the Slave States has been carelessly said of the Free. In the Free States probably labour is more honoured, idleness more despised, than in any other country in the world. Very rare are the instances, if my observation was correct, of men, however wealthy, who are merely living in luxury on their riches and adding nothing to the common store. As in Italy of old, so in America now, the merchant, however large the fortune he may have secured, seems almost always to retain his connection with commerce ; and like the Bardi, the Pitti, and the founders of the house of Medici, to act as a chief of industry and trade. However high men have risen, they are proud to own that it was by labour, even manual labour, that they rose. To have split rails with his own hands was in the eyes of Northern men a proud addition to Mr. Lincoln's escutcheon, and a recommendation to the highest office in the State. That the American community is immensely wealthy, its bitterest enemies cannot deny ; and if labour were not honoured, whence could the wealth come ?

In Europe divisions of class are sharp, as we feel to our cost whenever any political or social question is approached. And they run all down the scale. The farmer is an aristocrat, too often a very haughty aristocrat to the labourer ; the great tradesman to the small. And each class is ever dreading the claims and struggling against the pretensions of those beneath it. In America class divisions, though by no means extinct, are comparatively faint, and the jealousies and dangers which they entail are mitigated in proportion. All are politically equal, all are comparatively on a level in education and even in pro-

C

perty; any man may rise rapidly, and numbers are daily
rising from the lowest round of the ladder to the chief
places in commerce and the highest honours of the State.
Equality, therefore, is the rule of life. It is the rule, as
inequality is with us, throughout society. The farm
labourer lives as an equal at his employer's table, and I
have seen very well-dressed children, the children I was
told of wealthy parents, in school with the shoeless children of the emigrant. Perhaps in outward things the
rule is sometimes carried to a superstitious excess, which is
apt to provoke an inward reaction, as the outward deference
exacted by rank does here. But on the whole I am
persuaded that it is a happy rule. The fusion of classes
fills society with a feeling of security, not so familiar here.
It opens a wider and more varied range of social enjoyment, and better opportunities for the formation of social
character to every right-minded man. I cannot conceive
any countervailing benefits which an exclusive class, set
on an eminence by itself, can either receive or confer.
I know there are rich men in America who feel that
wealth is not enough honoured, and who, while they
conform to equality in public, recoil from it in secret, and
are glad to come over to European society for comfort. It
may be that wealth suffers a little there from the reaction
of feeling after its domination here. But, on the whole, I
confess it seemed to me that supposing a rich man to be a
man of sense and capable of deriving enjoyment from the
public welfare, equality added at least as much to his hap-
piness as to that of the poor.

The relations between employer and employed again,
so far as I could gather, though not free from difficulty or
discord, are upon the whole sounder and more kindly than

in this country. Strikes were rare till the derangement of prices caused by the Legal Tender Act put the world of industry out of joint. They were generally the new comers from Europe, I was told, who resorted to violent modes of raising wages ; the native American workman, in whom the real tendency of the community appears, usually taking, in case of difference, a more rational and amicable course. There seems to be an approach on the whole to an adjustment of mutual rights between the two classes less by the the angry clash of adverse interests and more by intelligence and the common sense of justice. And, if it be so, assuredly this is in itself a sufficient cause for wishing well to the great community of labour which is tracing out for us the better way.

The Irish form a low and dangerous class. But this dark stream of barbarism has its shameful source, not in America, but in misgoverned Ireland. America receives as much of it as she can in her common schools, finds it work and good wages, civilises it, and, not without trouble and peril to herself, converts the Irish pauper into an orderly and thriving citizen. It is an office for which, if we were disposed to be grateful to her, we shall owe her some gratitude. The last news I heard in this country, before embarking for America, was that of the Belfast riots. The dominant church of the minority and the oppressed church of the people were tearing each other to pieces in the name of religion. The effects of this, and of the alien land system which we persist in maintaining in Ireland, on the Irish character are seen again upon the other side of the Atlantic, but they are not to be charged upon American institutions.

One observes, indeed, in America, a sort of aristocracy

of races. The native American, with the English and Scandinavian immigrants, being at the head of the industrial scale; the Irish and the Southern Germans at the bottom : but it is a beneficent aristocracy, under which the lower races are being constantly trained by a necessary tutelage to the level of the higher.

The native American, generally speaking, is unwilling, from independence of feeling, as well as on account of the high remuneration of industry, to become a domestic servant; and that part is usually filled by the Irish. The consequence is a difficulty in getting good servants, which to most people from Europe seems a fatal defect in the structure of American society. The evil, however, if it be one, extends to our own colonies. This scarcity of servants leads to more self-help, more contrivances for supplying the place of servants' hands in houses, the total absence of large establishments, a great reduction of the number of persons out of the whole population whose labour is expended in waiting on the rich. Whether it may not lead to some more radical changes in the whole system of domestic servitude, and whether these changes will be beneficial to society or otherwise, remains yet to be seen.

The rate of wages which has been noticed as in part the cause of the scarcity of domestic servants, gives rise generally to a multitude of inventions for replacing manual labour by machinery. And this again tends to raise the condition of the labouring man. From being himself a machine, or, in the expressive phrase, a hand, he becomes the skilled manager of a machine. As these American inventions find their way to Europe, the same effect will, in some measure, be produced here. Skilled labour will be required by agriculture in place of unskilled, and the condition of our labourers will be raised.

It is a special mark of a Christian as distinguished from a heathen community, to care for all its members, not only for those who can maintain themselves and contribute to the general welfare, but for the sick, the infirm, and even for the criminal. America is the land of benevolent institutions, to which not only much money but a more precious tribute of voluntary labour is paid. It is the land too of mild criminal legislation and of prison reform. In its charities and in its model prisons, as well as in the opulence and comfort of its prim Quaker streets, Philadelphia stands a noble monument of the Society of Friends. Whether the system employed for the regeneration of the criminal has been in all things wise is a different question. There is no doubt such a thing as pseudo-philanthropy ; though it would be well if those who have denunciations of pseudo-philanthropists always in their mouths, would tell us, and show us by their own example, what genuine philanthropy is, that we may not be in danger of relapsing altogether into savagery and barbarism. But at all events, the system is an attempt to redeem the most abject, and at the same time often the most sorely tempted and the most unfortunate portion of humanity ; it is a genuine victory of the Christian spirit over those cruel fears which lead society to be lavish of punishment. Democratic justice, as well as philanthropy, contributed to the change. Our criminal law, in the last century, was the law of a privileged class, which hanged the rabble wholesale for petty larceny, while it indulged itself freely in duelling and all the vices of a gentleman. It is true that the benevolence and humanity, unquestionably characteristic of American nature, are partly virtues of prosperity—qualities not of character but of circumstance. The same people who are

so charitable to those in need, and so unwilling to inflict
cruel punishments on the guilty, are often criminally reckless of human life in the pursuit of gain. But it is thus
that human virtue finds its feet, propped by circumstance,
before it learns to stand by moral force alone.

Americans are supposed to be slaves to money. It is
true that many Americans are slaves to money, and are
hurried by the eagerness with which they pursue it through
lives of unrest into early graves. It could scarcely be
otherwise when human covetousness was excited by the
opening wealth of a new world. It is not wonderful that
the looks of the throng should be keener, and their steps
more hurried in the mart of New York than in the mart
of London. Nor is it wonderful that such immense opportunities for speculation should lead to commercial
gambling, and this again to a looseness of commercial
morality in certain circles—to what extent I must leave it
to commercial men to say, though it cannot be to so great
an extent as is often asserted, otherwise credit, and with
credit trade, would cease. The evil, I believe, is at least
as rife in our colonies as in the United States. But as
among the merchants of Florence, in old times, so in
America, the wealth which is eagerly and laboriously
made is generously spent, and often on public objects. A
successful trader in an aristocratic country buys a great
estate, and founds a noble family : a successful trader in
America founds a public institution. The great Italian
republic never poured out her wealth more freely in her
gallant struggles for the independence of Italy against the
tyrants of Milan, than did the merchants of the North in
struggling against the slave-owner for American freedom.
That commerce must be mean is a feudal superstition ;

less meanness commonly goes with the wealth that has been earned by labour than with that which is inherited and not earned. There is, if I mistake not, many a spirit among the great merchants of America as magnificent as that of any Cosmo or Lorenzo, though the magnificence of the American may not yet be guided by the same taste as that of the Florentine. Nor is wealth the thing, generally speaking, most worshipped by American society. Intellectual distinction is generally most worshipped. No owner of millions would have had the reception given to Mr. Dickens. The worship of intellect may itself be foolish and even wrong, it may be ill-directed, and assume ridiculous and repulsive forms. But it is a different thing from the worship of wealth.

Where wealth is luxury will be. Where wealth is suddenly made by men of little education or refinement luxury will be coarse. No doubt among the wealthy upstarts of New York and other great cities, sensualism, unregulated by taste, does assume its coarsest, most repulsive, and, therefore, perhaps least dangerous form. No doubt the world of mock-fashion in America does justly excite the scorn and disgust of the real world of fashion in Europe. I have seen myself figures which would have moved laughter in an English pantomime. But among the people of the better sort, however wealthy, I found, together with the greatest hospitality, genuine simplicity of life. The very scarcity of servants keeps ostentation, at all events, within bounds; and public opinion is opposed to a display of wealth, partly, it may be, from democratic jealousy, but partly, as I think, from feelings of a better and a more Christian kind.

Again, Americans are said to be wanting in courtesy.

That there are many discourteous people in America we may be sure ; and as aristocracy is apt to beget the rudeness of insolence, so democracy is apt to beget the rudeness of self-assertion. But though a student may not be a very shrewd observer of manners, or entitled to much attention on that subject, I must say, that wherever I went in America, whether I was among friends or strangers, I found myself among a kind and essentially courteous people. Never, when seeking information, or any of those good offices which a man in a strange country is sure to need, did I fail to meet with politeness and attention. No doubt to secure courtesy in America you must cordially accept equality; but in what community is it not necessary cordially to accept the leading principle of society if you wish to be courteously treated ? Manners in a certain sense are free. You are not required to put on a dress coat when you dine with a friend. But as a general rule, it did not seem to me that there was among Americans a want of mutual respect, or an unwillingness to pay reasonable deference to real social claims of any kind. In truth, equality is the necessary condition of courtesy in the proper sense of the word. Where there is a difference of social rank there may be condescension on one side and homage on the other; but courtesy can only exist between equals. The respect for women in America is notoriously carried to a height which some observers have even pronounced to be absurd, and injurious to the grace of the female character itself; though if this be so, like other exaggerations of untrained sentiment, it will find its level in course of time. I have been told that among the rural democracy of New England you may see the rudiments of finer manners than aristocracy ever produced. He who told me this was an

enthusiastic lover of his country. Yet I am not prepared
to say that his statement was untrue till I have seen more
of the American people. And if my credulity is thought
absurd, I must appeal from those travellers who have lived
in American hotels and steamboats to those, much fewer I
suspect in number, who have lived in American homes.

It is often asserted that family relations are bad in the
United States, that there is a want of filial affection and a
want of attachment to home. That this is not always the
case my own eyes are witnesses. No English home can be
better or more beloved than some in which I have passed
happy days in that country. That it is often the case
in America, as well as in Europe, I can easily believe. I
can easily believe, too, that in this case again, the excess
of the democratic spirit is partly the cause of the evil,
by enfeebling domestic authority and disparaging that
modesty in youth which is the only portal to dignity of
character in later years. But the independent manners
of children arise, in some measure at least, from their being
really independent of their parents, by beginning to earn
their own bread so young. In our own colonies the same
thing is seen, and the same complaints are made. And, if
affection does not centre so much in the old hearth of
the family, it is because in a new country, where the
people are still half-emigrant, old hearths are not so
common. Even here, our pictures of Christmas gather-
ings are drawn more from the mansions of the upper
class than from the cottages of poorer families who have
once dispersed in quest of bread. Besides, our sentiment
on these points is a little too absolute. Some change must
inevitably take place in these, among other relations, as the
world moves on. The domestic tie must to some extent

be superseded by the social. You cannot preserve in a
modern community the domestic exclusiveness of the
patriarch's tent.

The morality of a nation, in the restricted sense of the
term, is a point on which it is extremely difficult to speak
with accuracy in the case of any nation. The difficulty is
enhanced in the case of America, by the confusion of emigrant morality with that of the natives; the blending of
which two elements renders it also peculiarly hard to read
aright the statistics of crime. In a great commercial city
such as New York there is sure to be plenty of vice,
though the outward decency of that city, as you pass
through its streets by night, strongly contrasts with the
indecency of London. In no country, however, I believe,
is the marriage-tie, on the whole, more reverenced or more
strictly kept. Early marriage, which the circumstances of
the people permit, and which appears to be almost universal, must in itself be a great safeguard against the evils of
which moralists and social reformers are complaining here.
Infanticide, that hideous ulcer of our society, to the existence of which we have been terribly awakened, but which
we scarcely dare to probe, could hardly be very prevalent
in a land where children are almost an unmixed blessing.
There being no primogeniture, there are no younger sons
brought up in habits of luxury, and without the means of
marriage. All human virtue is comparative, and it appears that the sanitary records of the American army
denote comparative virtue. Of this I feel sure, that vice
which shows a bold front in the high places of society here,
would shrink abashed from public opinion in the United
States.

In a country where all the people have, from the rate

of wages, an almost unlimited command of drink and stimulants, habits of coarse indulgence are sure to be too common. This is naturally the case in an especial manner among the emigrants, unaccustomed to the command of such luxuries, and untrained to self-control. Popular effort, however, to reform popular vice is more common than it is with us. The Maine liquor-law may not have been wise or very effective, but it denotes a desire on the part of the masses to exert self-control ; and I am inclined to think that we shall see this desire further displayed.

I have not said, in touching on each of these main features of American society, this is a Christian feature ; but the remark would suggest itself spontaneously if what I have said on each point is true.

I speak of the political institutions last, not because they are the least important subject, but because this is the natural order. Political institutions are the expression of national character, though they re-act powerfully on the character, of which they are the expression. No community but one of diffused property and intelligence, socially united and sound in its morality, could support perfectly free institutions on so large a scale. Not the special form of the government, but the comparative absence of necessity for government, is the thing to be noted and admired, politically speaking, in the United States. The proper sphere of government is compulsion. The necessity for it in any given community is in inverse proportion to the social virtue and the intelligence of the people. The policeman, the executioner, the tax-gatherer, these are its proper ministers, and the representatives of what we call its majesty. It is destined to decrease as Christianity increases, and as force is superseded by social affection, and spontaneous

combination for the public good. The more a community
can afford to dispense with government the more Christian
it must be; and no great country has yet been able to dispense with government so much as America.

No man of any depth of character will worship democracy any more than he will worship monarchy or aristocracy. All alike are embodiments of force : monarchy is
the rule of one over all; aristocracy, of the few over the
many ; democracy, of the many over the few. An unjust
democracy is perhaps the most deeply wicked of all governments, because so many must be implicated in the
injustice. It is a fearful moral evil, compared with which
a tyranny may be almost regarded as a physical visitation.
And, at the best, democracy, like the other forms of
governnment, has special vices of its own : it is beset by
faction, by corruption, by popular passion, by demagogism,
by envious ostracism of merit, by oppression of classes
which are not numerically strong. American democracy
has not been free from these things, or from the odious
self-worship of the sovereign people. We have already
glanced at the bad influence, flowing from the same source,
which is visible in social and domestic life. I can well
understand that men of dignified and refined character
may shrink from politics, and wish, as the philosopher says,
" to stand under the wall while the cloud of dust whirls
by ;" though I cannot deem it the greatest of evils that the
highest intellect of the country should not be devoted to
work which, under ordinary circumstances, is very far from
being the highest. The evil has been aggravated by the
revolutionary bias given to the national character through
the rupture with the English monarchy, by the influx of
French Jacobinism in connection with the same event,

and by the error, as I presume to think it, committed by
the founders of the constitution, in imitating the great
centralised goverments of military Europe, and creating
an elective presidency which, with the patronage it com-
mands, must be the prize and the stimulant of intrigue,
faction, and personal ambition. It would be difficult to
stand at Washington, amidst the abortive streets of that
factitious capital, and not to feel that they are typical of a
great political misconception. What Providence intends
in the New World apparently is not a mere reproduction
of the European nations on a colossal scale, but a great
development of humanity, for which Federation, with its
infinite power of expansion, its multiplied centres of independent life, its freedom of local action, seems to be the
destined mould. It appeared to me that so far as American
institutions were local, they were good : good, at least, in
full proportion to the virtue, or, to speak plainly, to the
Christianity of the people in the state or district, and no
institutions can be more. The town meetings, where the
people manage their own affairs, and which form the solid
basis of American politics, are probably the soundest institutions in the world. Nearly as much may be said of
the State legislatures in the better States. It is in the
central government that such evil as there is has hitherto
had its main seat. There are the prizes for which the great
parties, with all their tyrannical and unpatriotic organisations, are formed. There are the "spoils" which, according
to the evil saying of Jackson, "belong to the victor" in the
unhallowed strife. There the great infirmity of all representative systems makes itself fully felt. The people would
generally chose the best candidate, if he were placed before
them. In the choice of the candidates lies the difficulty.

The readiest to come forward are not the best men, but those who most desire the prize ; and the selection is practically made by a party machinery which is apt to preclude all freedom of choice, and to force upon the electors the most violent partisan. Washington, itself a mere political and official city, removed from all the tempering influences of general society, seems the inevitable scene of cabal and corruption. I do not shut my eyes to these things. But it must be remembered that the action of the central government is in ordinary times very limited, and that the evils connected with it by no means sink deep into American life.

Again, I do not shut my eyes to the evils of universal suffrage, when extended not only to the educated and prosperous American, owning property or receiving high wages, and fully competent to exercise all the powers of a citizen, but to the ignorant and penniless emigrant, Irish or German. This is a mischief which has arisen from the desire in each state to create a large number of voters, that it may be largely represented in the central government. Possibly the increased firmness of tone which has been produced in American politics by this struggle, and the evidence which the Irish have given of their political character, may lead to some salutary measure for the preservation of the franchise from abuse, and for preventing these wanderers, while still in their uncivilised state, from destroying with their own hands the blessings which, when civilised, they are destined to enjoy. Meantime it is a fallacy, derived from the too exclusive study of New York correspondents of our newspapers, to suppose that the Irish mob of the great cities governs America. It might almost as well be said that the Irish

mob of London and Liverpool governs England. The
Irish, though they carry the city, cannot carry the state
of New York. The power of the country, as well as the
largest portion of its worth, in the last resort resides in the
yeomen, who, when a real emergency calls, can always be
trusted to come forward in overwhelming force, and
with a truly patriotic spirit, to guard the great interests of
the country.

Hitherto, however, there has been another disturbing
element, more serious than Irish violence itself, and one
for which the free institutions of America are as little
responsible as they are for Irish character. We must
suspend our judgment of the American government till
we have seen it fairly at work under better auspices than
those of the Democratic party. The two presidents of the
Republican party whom we have seen augur well for the
political future.

English notions of the political character of the Americans are naturally formed mainly from the American
journals, or rather they are formed from the worst passages
of the worst of those journals, carefully extracted for the
English market. The spirit of political journalism in
America is necessarily in the main that of the central
institutions, and it often enough gives one occasion to
raise the question as to the benefits of an anonymous
press. It does this not least when it is immolating the
character of other nations to the self-esteem of the American people. The writing is, generally speaking, inferior
to ours; the calling of a journalist not being so distinct or
so well paid there as it is here. I will venture, however,
to say that there is nothing in American journalism so
profligate or so coarse that a match may not easily be found

for it in the most aristocratic journals of this country. The United States having, fortunately for them, no real metropolis, there is no metropolitan press ruling the opinion of the whole country, and itself liable to the secret influences of the central government and of the circles of the capital. Nor is the press in America so poweful either for good or evil as it is here. The government being itself the authentic organ of the popular will does not stand so much in awe of self-constituted tribunes of the people.

Without a master, without a governing class, this great community is a law to itself. That it is, indeed, a law to itself, that American freedom is not anarchy, anyone who has seen the country must know. If the persons and the property of men were not secure, how could industry thrive? Whence could the wealth arise? In no monarchy or aristocracy, I venture to say, is the reverence for law among the people so deep. If you asked Americans for what they were fighting, nine out of ten would tell you that they were fighting to vindicate the law. And surely a great community which is a law to itself is a glorious thing : not only in itself, but still more in what it denotes. It marks a great step in the progress of humanity. It marks a great advance in the influence of Christianity. It confirms the Christian's faith in man.

There had been nothing like it before in history. Greece and Rome, though incomparably superior in their moral and intellectual productions to the monarchies of the.East, though presenting in the intensity of their patriotism the narrow prototype of an ampler fellowship to come, were, as was said before, really republics of masters, the mass of the people being slaves. The free cities of Italy, of Germany, of Flanders, produced in virtue of their freedom fruits of civilisation, as well as of industry, far nobler and more abundant than those which were produced by great feudal kingdoms. But their liberties were mere burgher liberties, deeply tainted with the tyranny of guild over guild, of city over city, of the inhabitants of the cities over the peasantry beneath their sway; based upon no broad principles of equity or respect for human rights, and doomed by their vices to an extinction which we mourn for the sake of art, but which we cannot call unjust. Nor had these municipalities ever entirely cast off the idea of allegiance to a suzerain, or pronounced in unfaltering accents the name of freedom. The republicanism of Switzerland was rather a geographical accident than an effort of humanity to rise to a nobler state; and this also was deeply tainted with aristocracy and with the domination of canton over canton. The republic of Holland was the noble but transient offspring of a rebellion against a foreign master, whose tyranny provoked resistance and whose overthrow left the provinces for a time without a sovereign. The nation of the Old World which has approached most nearly to a commonwealth, though under monarchial and aristocratical forms, is that of which, in the hour when the love of the public good was strongest in the hearts of its citizens and their political character at its grandest elevation, the American Republic was born.

In its external relations, also, the American commonwealth was a new birth of time. It kept no standing army, and, as far as the Free States were concerned, cherished no thought of conquest, though the military spirit had been excited, and a somewhat thrasonical element introduced into the national education and character by the first Revolutionary war. It was the Democratic

D

party, under Southern leaders, that made the war of 1810, which was resisted by the best spirits of the North. It was the South that dragged the Union into the attack upon Mexico. Every aggression—every scheme of aggression—was Southern. From Southern politicians installed at Washington proceeded all the insolent menaces and all the maxims of violence which have been so carelessly visited on the heads of their opponents and successors.

Grow the American Federation must. Its people know that it must grow : and diplomacy will do well at once to acquiesce in the natural and inevitable course of things. But the growth will be that of peaceful expansion and attraction; not of forcible annexation, of which I believe no considerable party at the North dreams or has ever dreamed. The British North American colonies will in time, and probably at no very distant time, unite themselves politically to the group of states, of which they are already by race, position, commercial ties, and the characteristics of their institutions a part. No one can stand by the side of the St. Lawrence and doubt that in the end they will do this; but they will be left to do it of their own free will.

Even as regards the Indians, it will be found, I believe, that it is on the South, not on the North, that the blame of the most flagrant aggressions rests. By the New Englanders greater and more sincere efforts were made on the whole to reclaim and Christianise these tribes than have been made by colonists in the case of any other savage race. But here disturbing influences from an extraneous source came in. Towards the close of the seventeenth century England and France went to war, armed the savage tribes on both sides in their American dependencies, and

put an end to the work of civilisation which down to that
date religion and philanthropy had not unhopefully carried on. Before that time there had been only two wars
between the New Englanders and the Indians in half a
century. A spirit more akin to that of Eliot and Penn is
now again in the ascendant, and a fresh hope dawns for the
Indian tribes.

No doubt American society, like European society, has
its peculiar evils. It has some which even a foreign
observer sees, and many more, we may be sure, which a
foreign observer does not see, but which Americans themselves know and feel, and which give birth to political and
social complaints there as mournful in tone as any that are
heard here. It is not by sudden and vigorous bounds, but
by slow and tottering steps that humanity advances.
Probably in many things the balance, here inclined too
much one way, is there inclined too much the other way,
and needs time and training to adjust it to the point
of perfect equity. Such of the national virtues as are
virtues of circumstance, have yet to be proved in a
severer school; while of the faults and absurdities some
at least are those of youth, and as the nation advances
in years will pass away. After all America is not a new
world, but the embryo of a new world. Many things
deemed peculiar to it are common to all colonies, and will
be modified as the colony becomes a nation. Of the
energy of the people, hitherto almost absorbed in the work
of reclaiming a continent, a larger share will be spared
for learning, art, and science. With higher cultivation
finer tastes will be introduced, vulgarity will be purged
away, extravagance will be chastened, more independent
intellects will arise, and the servility of thought, of which

there are just complaints at present, will cease to prevail. The restless movement westward will come to a stand. More settled habits and associations will be formed. A sounder and more effective philosophy will lay its tranquillising hand on the feverish pulse of political and commercial life. If justice prevails here, Ireland will become a home to her own people, and Irish emigration will cease to flow in so dangerous a current. The volume of emigration generally will perhaps be diminished, if governments in Europe grow wiser; and the American people, as a whole, will wear less the aspect of new comers still hastening on to fresh abodes. The habits of man will be better adapted to the climate of that continent, and a limit will be set to the nervous excitability produced by it, the influence of which is at present great, and more important, perhaps, in its effects than is generally supposed. At the same time new elements and influences will come into play, as the vast federation of the North American continent, the colossal lineaments of which are at present but faintly discernible, begins to assume its perfect form. The centre of power and importance will be transferred, as it is now fast shifting, to the mighty West. The federal institutions framed for the thirteen old colonies can hardly fail to undergo some change. The infant nation has hitherto been in many things like a child in an untouched orchard of nature, filling its arms with golden fruit, and letting them drop again as it hurried on to the next bough. The boughs, though laden, will be stript in time, the boundary of the orchard will be reached, the manhood of the nation will come, and bring with it new cares and perhaps difficulties as yet unforeseen. But the past can never return : Feudalism, Primogeniture, State Churches, are left behind for ever. Here was at all events a grand experiment; here was, for the first time, a great community, founded on the free allegiance of all its members to the common good; here was a great hope of Humanity, its newest and probably its fairest hope, though hope is not fulfilment, and though they to whom it is committed are human.

But effort is the law of the world. No hope reaches its fulfilment—no character, whether of man or nation, is formed without a struggle. For the American commonwealth, in its turn, a great trial was prepared.

If New England was, in the language of its founders, emphatically a plantation, not of trade but of religion; Virginia was as emphatically a plantation, not of religion but of trade. It was a plantation of gold-seekers, recruited by convicts. Afterwards there were added a few Cavaliers: but those who wish for Cavaliers should seek them rather in the poor white population of Barbadoes, whither they were exported in great numbers by Cromwell. The aristocracy of the South sprang from a different source. In Virginia and her sister States, partly from the climate, partly and principally from the character of their colonists, Slavery fixed its abode. By a fatal compromise with evil, sure, if God is strong and just, to bring down in the end a full measure of retribution, it was received into the constitution of the new Republic—received by men who had the highest doctrines of liberty and equality on their lips, and had just vindicated their own rights as freemen with the sword. But then it wore the harmless aspect of an aged and sickly man, whose life could not be brought at once to a violent close, but who would soon die in the course of nature. In those days the production of cotton by slave labour was unprofitable. The cotton gin was invented; the production of cotton by slave labour became a source of immense profit; opinion at the South, if it had ever been sincerely in favour of abolition, (which in spite of the loud professions of Southern Republicans is somewhat doubtful), underwent a complete change. That which had before been an evil, doomed to speedy extirpation, became inevitable, good, divine. A whole group of theological and philosophical theories sprang up to prove that what covetousness desired, God had decreed; and to show what intellectual feats hypocrisy can achieve when it is stimulated by the love of gold. And soon casting off the disguise of age and mortal sickness, under which he had crept into the commonwealth, the Demon towered up in colossal strength, and laid his terrible hand on the moral life of the American people.

As Northern society was in its structure and principles essentially Christian, Southern society was as essentially anti-Christian, and at the same time and for the same reasons essentially barbarous, though it might profess, and even unctuously profess, a belief in the Christian creed; though it might keep a Christian clergy to preach Slavery; though perhaps, if Secession had won the day, it would have had an Established Church for the same purpose. In its slave code it denied the fundamental principles of Christianity. It was in a literal sense based upon iniquity. Hideous as was its cruelty, at least as hideous and as subversive of Christian morality was its lust. It denied to its victim the conditions alike of moral and of intellectual manhood. It denied him what the worst of heathen slave states had not denied him, the hope of emancipation. For the purposes of its rapacity and pride, it was systematically effacing the image of the Creator from several millions of human beings, and this not without religious pretences, not without prayer. Almost as degrading to the poor whites as to the negro—morally, perhaps, even more degrading—it immolated the whole community to the vicious ends of a few wealthy men. Against the distinct command of Christianity, it branded labour with dishonour; and within its pale the meanest white preferred a life of penury, wandering, sponging on the great planters, to honest industry—the lot and badge of the negro slave. Instinctively hating the light which Christianity loves, as well as dreading the growth of intelligence in the slave or in the dependent white, it excluded popular education and every source of popular enlightenment; and when Secession had fairly let loose its tongue, it spoke of them openly with devilish hatred. By brutalising labour, it often blasted the fertility of the very soil which it occupied, and the forest is seen growing in Virginia over the traces of ancient cultivation. Pretending to set intellect free from manual toil and to dedicate it to higher ends, it produced no intellectual fruits whatever, except a statecraft, the sole object of which was to maintain and propagate Slavery. It could not produce intellectual fruit, because the noble aspirations which lead to the discovery of truth, the tenderness which creates intellectual beauty, could not dwell with brutality and injustice. The traveller in its realms found no books, no musical instruments, no means of culture. It generated a barbarism, the deeper because it was not original but relapsed, which met the civilisation of the Free States on the boundary line between them, like a dark element meeting a brighter, and was plainly depicted on the very faces of the Southern soldiery. It was full of violence and bloodshed, of stabbing, duelling, and lynch law, the offspring of the passions fostered by domestic tyranny. So jealously was the den of Slavery closed and its mysteries concealed, that till the Northern armies penetrated into the South, the horrors of the system were not fully known. Not the mutual confidence which reigns at the North, and produces there an almost reckless freedom of social intercourse, but suspicion, bred of conscious wrong, brooded over the realm of Slavery. The face of every stranger was scrutinised, his words and demeanour watched. Nor was silence enough : to a public conscience so burdened, silence was a reproach ; you must speak in favour of slavery, or feel its knife. No doubt there was lavish hospitality, such as brought golden words from those who shared it, in the houses of Southern planters, as there always is where prodigality is fed by the sweat of another man's brow. No doubt the graces of Southern ladies often won them admirers and partisans ; so did those of the Roman ladies who were in the habit of crucifying slaves. The proudest of aristocracies, this society was called. Let those who gave it that name cease to accuse others of traducing aristocratic institutions.

As a power, Slavery was, and would always have been, fiercely aggressive. It ravened for land to supply the place of that which its ruinous culture had exhausted, and it could not bear the reproachful and contagious neighbourhood of free institutions. While it ruled the foreign policy of the States, that policy was always menacing and piratical. The North could not have lived at peace with it ; England could not have lived at peace with it, unless she had sunk, as some of her sons would have had her sink, to to the level of its degradation.

There had been no iniquity like it before. The Slave States of antiquity sinned, and their sin was their death ; but they did not sin in the light, and therefore their corruption was less deep. The idea of a common humanity transcending all divisions of tribe and race had in those times scarcely dawned upon the mind of man, and the pang of conscience was hardly felt in reducing men of another tribe or race to Slavery. There was even a kind of justice in Slavery as it then existed. In an age of universal war the slave, while he sustained the community by his labour, was exempted from the dangers and hardships of military service, which it was the lot of every freeman to undergo. And, moreover, Roman Slavery became in its later days a great channel both of education and of emancipation.

The political character of the Southern Oligarch however was closely akin to that of the slave-owning republicans of antiquity, little as he resembled them in their culture and their classic grace. It was full of the same rebellious pride, the same fierce spirit of self-assertion, combined with the same haughty contempt for the rights of others. The land of slavery was the land of tyrannicide. *Sic semper tyrannis* was the motto of Virginia ; and every one was a tyrant who restrained the tyranny of the slave-owner. The patriotism of the North, so far as it approaches its ideal, is that of a Christian community ; the patriotism of the South was that of a heathen republic.

And the great political quality of the slave-owning republic was to be its stability. It was to remain for ever unchanged, while all things were in a state of change around it. Hope of piratical aggrandisement at the expense of its neighbours it had. Other hope it had none, either for the master or for the slave. The faith of that Christian community was faith in force, its charity Slavery, its hope despair.

The conflict between Slavery, thus erected into a powerful interest, and Freedom was irrepressible ; the phrase has become hackneyed, because it is so true. The struggle began in the political field, and was there waged through a series of party encounters, of which this civil war was in fact only the culmination. In the political field Slavery found an organisation ready made for it, and a weapon prepared to its hands in the Democratic party. Washington and his friends had fought as Englishmen for the great charter. But there was another party, of which Jefferson was the leader, an offset not of English patriotism but of French Jacobinism, and like its parent stock in irreligion, in canting philanthropy, in lust of violence and blood. This party made the war of 1810, and carried into power General Jackson, the American counterpart of the Dantons and Santerres. The party of Washington and Hamilton were for a strong federal government. In opposition to them the Democrats held the doctrine of state-right—a doctrine in itself respectable, and, as I believe, sound ; but held in an evil spirit, and perverted to evil ends. From this semblance of attachment to local and popular rights, it arrogated to itself the name Democratic. Under the organisation of this party the slave oligarchy extended itself. There it had as its allies and tools the lowest democratic element of the North, the Irish of New York and the other great cities, so that the worst spirit of oligarchy and the worst spirit of democracy were blended into a combination of evil as fell as ever menaced the the political life of a nation. The days of this party were

days of violence at home as well as abroad. They produced abroad the Ostend manifesto, at home that worst of
democratic excesses—the destruction of judicial independence by the institution of elective judges. Besides the
slave-owners and the Irish, the party embraced a number
of rich men at the North who sympathised socially with
the slave-owner, and a body of hereditary partisans, with
place-hunters not a few. The slave-owners were the
leaders of the whole; they fought for a principle, and
could afford to throw the pelf of office to their meaner
allies. Never has a name been so abused as that of democratic when applied to this confederation. Yet that name
stood the leaders in good stead. It drew to them, among
other reinforcements, a number of exiles from European
tyrannies for whom anything democratic had a charm.
The ends of the party were well defined. Its discipline
was perfect. It was led, like the Confederate armies in
the beginning of the war, by men accustomed to command.
It obtained complete possession of power, and established
a political reign of terror. Many things conspired in its
favour. The rapid growth of wealth was engendering a
disregard of principle; for after all it is really hard, as the
history of many a base surrender and betrayal has proved,
for a rich man to enter into the kingdom of heaven. The
interests of Slavery were supposed to be inextricably en-
twined with those of national wealth; the country was full
of its commercial partners and its creditors. Its enemies
became the enemies of the rich. From other causes faith
was decaying, and the power of moral resistance which
faith alone can sustain in extremity was growing weak.
Good society was all on the same side. The Churches
of the wealthier class, thinking no doubt that so long as

they held fast to orthodoxy they might let morality go, or
rather because they had no real faith in them, but only a
traditional creed, bowed, under the hypocritical pretence of
political neutrality, to the dominant iniquity of the hour.
Conspicuous among them in compliance was that Church—
the Church, as we have said, of wealth and fashion—the
presence of which in America appears to our High-Church-
men the only redeeming feature in that God-forsaken world.
Soon, even in New England, abolitionists were hunted
down as noxious fanatics; the rich, and, as they call themselves, the respectable citizens, heading the mob which
assailed them.   The moral life of the community was fast
ebbing away under the deadly pressure.   The national legis-
lature was gagged, and the press was in danger of being
gagged on the question most vital to the well-being of the
state.   Men do not yet know what a crisis in the world's
history this was.   The supreme moment seemed to have
come, when Daniel Webster, a puny soul in a giant body
of intellect, passed to the side of Slavery in hope of obtain-
ing the Southern nomination to the presidency, which, however, the mocking fiend denied him, when he had sold his
principles and his fame.   Humanity will for ever honour
the names of Theodore Parker and those who with him
struggled in this the darkest hour of American history, at
the cost of social excommunication, at the risk of personal
violence, to stem the mingled tide of Slavery, materialism,
and political atheism which was overwhelming the moral
world, and beneath which, as Parker says in his funeral
oration on Webster, everything had sunk, even the
steeples of the highest churches, except the ark of God.
Their indignation against dominant wrong may have provoked these men to the use of violent language.   Their

indignation against orthodox hypocrisy demurely pander-
ing to the wickedness of wealth and power, may have provoked them to the use of language offensive to piety. Our
criticism is easy, their struggle was hard.

It was not the opponents of Slavery, however, that
roused the North at last, but the slave-owners themselves.
Evil always contains in it the germ of its own destruction.
The tyrannical violence of the slave-owner carried him
beyond what subserviency could endure—his tendency to
aggression beyond what apathy could overlook ; while his
uneasy conscience led him to exact securities for his institution, which were effectual only in multiplying and exas-
perating his enemies. The fugitive slave-law was a final
appeal to whatever of morality and honour might linger in
the heart of the nation. A captured slave, dragged back
to the lash through the streets of a Northern city, was a
sight to make the stones cry out against the sufferance of
a debased people. Slavery, as it were, scourged on the
reaction which finally bore Mr. Lincoln into power; and
even Mr. Lincoln himself was in effect elected by the
slave-owners, who might, with their democratic allies in
the North have carried a moderate friend of Slavery, but
chose to split the party, and let an avowed enemy become
President, that they might have a pretext for civil war.
An avowed enemy to Slavery Mr. Lincoln was, and stead-
fastly, though by constitutional means, did he seek its
overthrow; yet he and his party, at the time of his election, hoped only for its territorial limitation. It was
Slavery itself that would be satisfied with nothing short
of its own destruction. The Kansas question had wound
up both parties almost to the war-pitch. The assault on
Mr. Sumner had already given the signal of violence. The
slave-owners sprang to arms.

We will not argue over again the question of constitutional law. What I have always said on that subject is,
that if there was a constitutional right of secession, of
which I can see no trace whatever in the language of the
Constitution, this was not an exercise of that right ; this
was a conspiracy as dark and treacherous, as deeply tainted
with abused confidence and betrayal of trust, as any conspiracy in history. The man who poisons his friend in the
cup of hospitality is not more perfidious than were the
public servants who used the power confided to them over
the public arsenals clandestinely to disarm the country, and
expose it defenceless to the meditated blow. But it may
be urged, there is a natural right of rebellion, independent of written constitutions, which no republican or Liberal
can gainsay. That there is a right of rebellion against
hopeless tyranny, for the purpose of recovering freedom, I
admit; I do not admit that there was a right of rebellion
against a free government, under which no grievance was
hopeless, for the purpose of making a great mass of its people slaves for ever. The negro-labourers of the South had
no part in secession ; it was made to rob them of their last
hope of emancipation, and they were entitled to the protection of the State : so were the white people of Western
Virginia and Eastern Tennessee, who, when they resisted
secession, were coerced by the slave-owners as rebels. Moreover, it is, I am convinced, a mistake to think that secession was a mere separation. It would have proved, and
the chief authors of the plot intended that it should prove,
indefinite aggression. Not only would the Slave Empire
have spread westwards and southwards over territories
destined to be the seat of great free communities, and of
the future of which the American commonwealth was the

trustee. As I am persuaded, the Confederacy was not intended to remain for ever bounded on the North by a frontier so close to its capital. The old alliance with the anti-republican rich and with the democratic mob of the North, those commercial interests and connections the strength of which had been so fatally proved, the standing army which the Slave Confederacy would certainly have kept up and with which it would always have been ready to interpose in favour of its political allies, would probably have brought over to it the Border States, Kentucy, Maryland, Missouri, already tainted with Slavery ; might possibly have brought over to it even Pennsylvania and New York, in both of which the Democratic and Pro-Slavery party was very strong : and the visions of restoring the right relation between labour and capital, (visions not confined to the case of the black labourer) might have been fulfilled in the city of William Penn, as well as over the grave of Washington and in the halls of the Incas. Christianity was not the aggressor in the conflict ; it was struggling for life. It did not even technically deal the first blow. The Northern people, with their government, were standing at gaze, not knowing how to act, unwilling to attempt coercion, ready, I am afraid, a good many of them, to avert disruption by concessions to Slavery, when Slavery, still impelled to suicide by the vices of its own character, fired on the national flag at Fort Sumter, and the North sprang to arms. The importance of that incident in rousing the Northern people to a spontaneous movement, which the government could not, if it would, have failed to obey, has not been understood here, nor has its effect upon the question as to the lawfulness of the war been duly weighed. When one of two parties begins a

war, it is surely lawful for the other to prosecute it to a
victorious issue, even though that issue may be not the
transfer of a province from one king to another, but the
transfer of a world from Slavery to Freedom. The em-
ployment of arms for the propagation of principles or
institutions is not to be justified. But this was a war to
save principles and institutions from armed aggression ;
it was not only a righteous but a defensive war.

It is needless to give a history of the great conflict, and
less to recall events and vicissitudes fresh in every memory,
and at which our hearts have scarcely ceased to throb.
The struggle was long, and its length made the extirpation of Slavery sure. Emancipation owes its completeness,
under Providence, to the tenacity of President Davis and
the skill of General Lee. The course of events remarkably
resembled, in some respects, that of our civil war in the
time of Charles I. The Federals, like the Parliamentarians, were superior in numbers and in wealth ; but they
were unwarlike in their habits, and wholly untrained to
command and obedience ; while the Confederates, like the
Cavaliers, were accustomed to carry arms and to exercise
command over their dependents, who again, from their
habits of life, were soldiers almost ready made. The
Federals began, like the Parliamentarians, with over-
weening confidence and humiliating failure. After Bull's
Run, after the failure of M'Clellan, the defeat of Pope,
the defeat of Burnside, shouts of exultation and derision
arose from the enemies of the Republic. The world laid
down its money with confidence on the Confederate side ;
and the hearts of all who hated freedom, civil or religious,
were filled with an unwonted joy ! The model Republic
had fallen ! To tyranny, to class privilege, to darkness,

after all belonged the future of mankind! But if the
slave-owners had the strength of an oligarchy, the Federals
had the far greater strength of a community, and in that
strength they conquered. For the sake of their community
they learned obedience in war, a more effective obedience
than that which the conscript yields under the lash. They
turned their vast industry to a new purpose, and produced
on a marvellous scale, with marvellous rapidity, and with
marvellous excellence, all the materials of war. They drew
military aptitude from all the grades of an educated and
intelligent community, and raised it to command. With
the power of voluntary association, which the members of
a real community alone possess, they aided their government in its new and colossal task. They sustained it
through all reverses, and in spite of all its errors, with the
loyalty which can be paid only by a real community to the
government of its choice. They animated it, and all who
under it fought or laboured for the common cause, with
the spirit of a united people. Gradually the resources of
the slave oligarchy began to fail. The conscription laws,
· to which almost from the outset it had been forced to
resort, though supported by the sternest military discipline, were ineffectual to keep its white serfs in the line.
It was compelled to tear the veil from its own hypocrisy,
and to ask the negro, to whom it had denied the rights and
the very name of man, to shed his blood as a fellow-
citizen for a common country ; though with a proviso that
if he conquered in the common cause the property of his
master in him should remain unchanged. The operations
of the Federals, now directed by officers of the highest
merit, were better combined, and pressed at all points on
the enemy, who before, by moving swiftly from point to

E

point in the inner circle, had beaten or baffled the Federal
commanders one by one. While Sheridan dealt blow after
blow in the Shenandoah Valley, while Grant held Lee
immovable before Richmond, while Farragut and Porter
thundered on the sea coast, another Federal army, under
Sherman, pierced through the circle of the military de-
fences into the heart of the Confederacy, and encountered
no popular resistance. This was the end. And never did
the moral and intellectual forces more signally prove their
ascendency over the physical forces in war. It is too late
to deny this now. It is too late now to affect wonder that
the Confederacy could hold out so long, after telling us
for four years, and persuading men to risk their money on
the faith of the prediction, that the task which the Federals
had undertaken was hopeless, and that the victory of the
Confederates was sure.

The greatest deliverances of Humanity have been
wrought by higher agencies than war. But by war no
such deliverance of Humanity was ever wrought as this.
Not the fields on which Greek intellect and art were saved
from the Persian; not the fields on which Roman law and ·
polity were saved from the Carthaginian and the Gaul; not
those plains of Tours on which Charles Martel rolled back
Islam from the heart of Christendom; not the waters over
which the shattered Armada fled; not Leipsic and Lutzen,
Marston and Naseby, where, at the hands of Gustavus and
Cromwell, the great reaction of the seventeenth century
found its doom, will be so consecrated by the gratitude of
after ages as Vicksburg and Gettysburg, Atlanta, and those
lines before Richmond which saw the final blow.

And how, on the whole, did the North bear itself in
this war? how did its love of law, its patriotism, its hu-

manity endure this, notoriously the severest test which
can be applied to the character of a nation ? The answer
to this question is as important as the actual issue of the
war.

There was to be an anarchy. So said that wisdom
which is wise by precedents, and which, in choosing its
precedents, is guided by its passions. Never, through the
whole of the conflict—fiercely as the passions of parties
were inflamed at the North—was public order seriously
disturbed, except by the savage Irish at New York ; and
on that occasion it was quickly seen that there was force
enough upon the side of order, and that the belief in
the omnipotence of the New York mob, however time-
honoured, was not true. I witnessed myself the last Presi-
dential election. No occasion could be imagined more
trying to the self control of the people. I said at the time,
and I repeat now, that the day passed off like an English
Sabbath. There was not, I believe, in all the States, as
much disturbance as, at the previous general election in
England, there had been in the rotten borough of Calne.
At New York only was there any apprehension even
of a breach of the peace : and there again it was the
Irish only that gave occasion for the fear. Some troops
were brought into the harbour ; but I believe they were
not landed : certainly they were not called upon to act.
The minority, even in the places where it was at once
weakest and most odious, was allowed to express its
sentiments on the the platform and through the press,
to hold its party meetings, to celebrate its torchlight pro-
cessions, to hang its banners across the public way un-
molested and unrebuked. I saw friendly greetings pass
between men of opposite parties, as they went to the

poll on the issue of which hung, as they believed, national
life and death. I saw, by proof still more conclusive,
that private courtesy survived—with difficulty perhaps,
but still it survived—the bitterest political estrangement.
Tyranny of opinion ! Too much of it no doubt there is
in America, and wherever else human nature has not
yet thoroughly learnt the highest and hardest of moral
lessons—perfect respect for conscientious difference of conviction. But the tyranny of opinion in America in the
midst of a dangerous civil war appeared to me, I confess,
very like the freedom of opinion which other countries
enjoy in time of security and peace.

After the anarchy, there was, as a matter of course, to
be a military despotism. It seemed, indeed, from the language used, that the two were existing at the same time.
Sages began to whisper in awful tones that the rule of
a military despot was the issue to which all the respectable
people in the United States were looking forward with
melancholy complacency as their only refuge from the horrors of freedom. The first successful general would, without fail, overturn the constitution ; and his army would,
without hesitation, make itself the instrument of his treason. And it must be confessed that this prediction had all
the precedents in its favour. Yet not a shadow of military
despotism ever fell upon the scene ; not a thought of trea-
sonable usurpation ever, so far as we can see, entered any
commander's mind. When, upon a single occasion, a
victorious general stepped beyond a general's province,
and assumed a power of negotiation which belonged only
to the civil government, his soldiers, though he was their
idol, showed at once that they had been citizens before
they were soldiers. These men, as has been pertinently

remarked, were readers; and when soldiers are readers, it
it is difficult to use them as Prætorians or Zouaves. The
fears, natural as they were, of the predominance of a military spirit, and of the ascendancy of the military over the
civil power, have so far proved totally unfounded; the
ascendancy of the civil power over the military has, on the
contrary, been maintained in a manner very memorable
and very full of comfort. No sooner was the war at an end
than the armaments were reduced; and the soldiers, who
were to be the tyrants of the country, returned not only
willingly but eagerly to their peaceful occupations; though
there were many officers, still young or in the prime of life,
who had half run a brilliant career, and in whom the
desire of completing that career must have been strong.
If a larger standing army than usual is still kept on foot,
it is partly because the fires of rebellion are hardly yet
extinct, partly on account of the threatening presence of
French ambition. General Grant himself is foremost in
all measures for reducing the standing army, and he it is
who, by his noble avoidance of military pomp and of
everything that could inflame the military spirit, and by the
magnanimity with which in his own person he has kept
the soldier in subordination to the citizen, has done most
to prevent military passions from gaining possession of the
nation, and to avert the danger, if ever there was any, of
sabre sway. He is greater in this than in his victories.
The Duke of Wellington was deemed a high example
of duty because, loaded with wealth and honours as the
reward of his services, he did not attempt to overturn
the constitution of his country, as Napoleon characteris-
tically took it for granted that he would. Let this standard
of conduct be applied to the American commanders, and

the characters of some of them will stand high. But in truth they must have had bad hearts to conspire against the liberties of their country: so rich is the reward of gratitude and affection bestowed by the American people on all who have served or tried to serve them well.

The President, during the struggle, necessarily exercised great power. He became by the tacit consent of the nation almost the Dictator of the imperilled Republic. At all times indeed the power of a President is greater than is commonly supposed ; and if the constitutions of England and America are compared with regard not to their forms but to their substance, that of America will be found to approach more nearly to a popular and elective monarchy, that of England to an aristocratic republic. With invasion on the frontier and treason swarming within it, a few arrests of doubtful legality and doubtful expediency were made ; but they were made without any unconstitutional design, and with a merely preventive object, to restrain the persons arrested from courses which might have led to the penalty of treason. Arbitrary things were done in some places by military subordinates unaccustomed to the exercise of power. But on the whole it may truly be said that in no country engaged in civil war, or even in imminent danger of invasion, have law and liberty been so little disturbed as they were, during this civil war, in the loyal states. At the South, meantime, Unionists, or men suspected of being Unionists, were being hunted down like wild beasts. After the murder of Mr. Lincoln, a disposition was shown by the Government to employ secret tribunals for the trial of his murderers ; but the nation, excited as it was against the authors of a great crime, declared at once for publicity as the safeguard of justice ; and from the time when the conflict ceased, law has resumed its uninterrupted course. To preserve the Constitution unimpaired was, throughout, the aim, almost the passion, of the man who was under the greatest temptations to impair it : and he succeeded, for not a particle of it has perished. That the proclamation of liberty to the negroes in the insurgent states was not an act of lawless tyranny but a fair measure of war, became clear to all when the insurgents began to use the slaves as soldiers.

If the Government showed respect for law, did not the people show respect for authority? Those who declaim on the fickleness of Democracy may be safely challenged to produce from history an instance of a government so followed and supported through such trials and reverses. Never for a moment, even when the failure of the war seemed most complete, and when the elections of the great state of New York were going against the Government, did the constitutional ruler fail to command the constitutional obedience of the citizen. A popular Government, of course, felt it necessary to entitle itself to allegiance by showing a reasonable respect for public opinion and a paramount regard for the public interest. When an officer had decisively failed in supreme command (never, I apprehend, before he had decisively failed), he was removed, and he immediately became in the eyes of aristocratic critics a victim of democratic ingratitude. But the victims of ingratitude continued, with perhaps one notable exception, to serve their country zealously in inferior posts. It is one of the noblest features of the struggle ; it speaks volumes for the beneficence of institutions, attachment to which can thus prevail over selfishness even in a case where selfishness so easily assumes the mask of dignity and self-respect.

The cohesion of the States again was, we were told, to give way under this strain. It was impossible that such a Government could be revered far from its centre, or that the Union could have advantages enough to hold together its distant members under any severe pressure. Every day the West was about to part from the East, as well as the South from the North; and instead of one disruption, if the war went on, there were to be a dozen. Yet not only did the West remain firm and true; but remote California rivalled her sisters in loyalty and zeal for what to her also was the common cause.

The soldiers of the North were described as hirelings—Irish and Germans selling their blood for Yankee gold. In those vast hosts there were many foreigners, though foreigners who for the most part intended, unlike our German Legion in the Crimean war, to make the country which they served their home. There were also many soldiers of Irish and German extraction, as in the British armies there are many Angles, Jutes, and Saxons, not to mention Normans and other men of alien ancestry not a few. But that the mass were American husbandmen, woodsmen, and artisans, the world must begin to believe, now that it sees them return to the plough, the axe, the workshop, and the loom. The armies of the South were raised, after the first year at least, by the most sweeping conscriptions, in which utter disregard was shown for public faith; men who had voluntarily enlisted for a year being voted in for a longer term, and at last to the end of the war. Those of the North were raised in a great measure, as the armies of European monarchies are entirely raised, by the inducement of pay; and the usual evils of recruiting, crimping and trepanning, did not fail to attend the process when the demand for recruits became great, especially in New York, where the people, though compelled to furnish their contingent, were at once peculiarly unwarlike, and mainly on the Southern side. The North, as an industrial community, fought as industrial communities (our own included) always fight, with the industry which supplies the sinews of war : and this became more apparent as the war went on, and the drain upon the labour market became more severe. But there must also have been many in the Northern armies to whom, the rate of wages and the earnings of industry being what they are in that country, the pay of a soldier could have been but a slight inducement. On the whole, probably no country has ever received a larger free-will offering of its children's blood. There were some at least in those ranks whose self-devotion (I hardly like to use the profaned name of chivalry) could scarcely be doubted. It was no sordid motive that led Mr. Wadsworth, when past middle age, to leave wealth, ease, social honour, troops of friends, for the hardships of a soldier's life, and death at the head of his division. It was no sordid motive which led Colonel Lowell, whose funeral I myself witnessed, to resign the pleasures of a fine and cultivated intellect and the brightest promises of opening life for the service in which he gloriously fell. It was no sordid motive and no common self-sacrifice that led Colonel Shaw to accept the command of the first negro regiment, and imperil not only his life, but his reputation, to redeem the despised race. When Colonel Shaw was killed in leading his regiment against Fort Wagner, the Southern chivalry, insulting the dead, buried him, as they said, among his *niggers*. A Federal general was about to remove the body to a more honourable place of burial : but Colonel Shaw's family desired that it might rest in that most honourable grave where it already lay. That rich and refined Americans are disaffected to the institutions of their country is a very common belief, to which the language of some of them when in this country lends colour. But I have seen rich and highly refined Americans, accustomed to the best society of Europe, rejoice as they approached their home, though that home was at the time the scene of civil war; and in this struggle not a few of that class gave noble proof (proof never to be forgotten by their countrymen) that the rich, as well as the poor, may be heartily loyal to the government of the people.

As the Americans were said to be shedding only the blood of hirelings, so they were said to be spending only the money of posterity. I will not be guilty of extenuating either the evils of a national debt, or the criminality of laying the burdens of the present generation on posterity, if the State can possibly be saved by any other means. The Americans have, unhappily, borrowed a great sum. Other nations, not only when fighting for existence, but when fighting for mere ambition, had done the same before them : but, unlike other nations, they seem disposed to make an effort to pay what they have borrowed ; and if they have burdened posterity, they have really secured it against war. They were doomed by their critics to be, or rather they were already, bankrupt. But now they have become a salutary example of a nation determining to reduce its debt; though the way in which they proceed to the reduction of the debt, by first reducing their armaments, is not so clearly perceived. Ignorant of finance, which had never been a pressing subject in a country without great establishments and heavy taxes, they committed at first some great financial errors ; above all the error of passing the Legal Tender Act, the consequences of which they still feel in the derangement of prices, the disturbance of trade, and the prevalence of gambling speculation in gold. Nor was the willingness of the people to bear taxation at first fully appreciated by the government itself. But towards the close of the war the whole amount of the burden, which it must be remembered was really self-imposed, including all the imposts, Federal and State, must have been as heavy as was ever borne : and at the same time large sums, as well as very precious time and labour, were being freely contributed to patriotic objects connected with the war.

In this, as in other respects, the character of the nation improved as the war went on. So again, at the outset, the immense amount of sudden expenditure, and the vast number of contracts thrown at once upon the market, no doubt bred, as such things always will breed, a great deal of roguery and corruption. But in time, reasonable purity, as well as efficiency, was secured ; so I was assured by informants unconnected with the administration, and who were not strong partisans of the war. That the Government itself was not actuated by the corrupt love of patronage, it has proved by its prompt reduction of the great establishments, on the magnitude of which its patronage depended.

There is a question more important still, especially to those who insist that the American community is based on Christianity. How did the humanity of the people bear the most terrible of all trials, the trial of civil war? To be able to answer this question fairly we must recall to our minds the records of other civil wars—those of the civil wars in France between the Burgundians and the Armag-

nacs, between the Huguenots and the Catholic League,
between the Royalists and Republicans at the time of the
Revolution, even between the party of Order and the
Reds in 1848—those of the civil wars between Guelfs and
Ghibelins, in the Italian cities—those of the Thirty Years'
War in Germany—even those, though far less dreadful, of
our own civil war in the time of Charles I., or of our
colonial war at the time of the American Revolution. If
we would be just—if we would avoid the deserved impu-
tation of hypocrisy and Pharisaism—we must also recall
to mind the severities with which we have thought it
lawful to put down rebellion in Ireland and India. Tried
by the historical standard, I am convinced that the
Federals will be found, on the whole, to have shown,
both in the war and after it, a humanity which may
be almost said to form an epoch in the moral history
of our race. Acts of ferocity and devastation were no
doubt committed by armies in the enemy's country;
and evil be to him who, whether from want of feeling or
from partisanship, speaks lightly of such things. The
houses of Confederates were ruthlessly burnt by Federals
on land, while the ships of Federals, even those engaged
in the most peaceful commerce, even the barks of harmless
fishermen, were being destroyed as ruthlessly by the Confederates at sea. But I feel confident that when the truth
shall have been sifted from the falsehoods purveyed by the
worthy agents of an unprincipled press for the gratification
of malignity here, it will be found that rarely if ever was
blood shed except on the field of battle; and that the
stories of women given up to the lust of the soldiery at
New Orleans and elsewhere, were unadulterated lies. The
proclamation of General Butler, in particular, which filled

with chivalrous indignation the bosom friends of Louis
Bonaparte, St. Arnaud, and Pelissier—those who had hung
the banner of Perjury and Massacre beside the banner of
the Black Prince, was bad in form, but in substance it
was merely a threat to women who insulted soldiers and
officers in the street, who spat in an officer's face, that they
should be treated as street-walkers were treated under the
local law. It proved effectual, and saved all the decent
women and all the decent citizens of New Orleans from the
consequences of a collision between the garrison and
the inhabitants.* No captured city of the Confederates
suffered the fate of Magdeburg or Lyons, or even of
Badajoz and St. Sebastian. I visited myself a large
prison camp and a prisoner's hospital. The inmates
of the prison camp were evidently well fed, and, so far as I
could see, were undergoing no hardship not inseparable
from a captive's lot. The inmates of the prison hospital
were treated, if my eyes did not deceive me, with the utmost liberality and kindness. The agents of the Sanitary
Commission, when they came upon a field of battle, made
no distinction between the wounded friend and the
wounded enemy. Public sentiment did not demand, and
would not have suffered any effective retaliation for the
atrocities of Andersonville. At the very time when the
North was ringing with the report of those atrocities, I was
able to write that though I had heard fierce expressions of
indignation against the rebels and of determination to put
them down, I had heard scarcely a single expression of
bloodthirstiness, scarce a single expression of desire for
vengeance. At the time, I believe what I said seemed

---

* Perhaps I may be permitted to say that I had satisfied myself of this
before I became General Butler's guest.

incredible. It will hardly be thought incredible now. For this great rebellion, by which the Commonwealth was brought to the verge of destruction, not a single life has been taken. Wirtz, the only man who has been executed, suffered not for his part in the rebellion, but for thousands of murders. Mr. Davis is still awaiting his trial; but nobody imagines that he will be put to death. Confiscation was suspended over the heads of the Southern oligarchy for a time : but they have suffered no personal punishment, though they have lost slavery, the stake of the desperate game which they had played with the blood of so many thousands. Oligarchs too must pay, when they play at rebellion and lose the game. The Southerners are called upon to accept the system which has been pronounced by overwhelming authority to be alone compatible with Christianity, morality, and industrial prosperity : this is the penalty which they have to undergo for the most criminal and dangerous attempt ever made not only against a single Commonwealth, but against the Commowealth of Man. There are some who doubt the wisdom of this all embracing mercy. It is as profoundly wise as it is noble and full of high instruction to mankind. Its wisdom will not be the less manifest, even though the South should fail to be touched by it, and provoke measures of severity, which then would have the moral approbation of the whole world.

We were led to believe that while the South was all dignity and self-sacrifice, the North was revelling in a ghastly and almost fiendish whirl of gaiety and dissipation. It no doubt was so among a certain set at New York, in the vortex of contracts and gambling speculation. But elsewhere I can bear witness that it was not. Elsewhere

I can bear witness that society wore an aspect not unbecoming a nation under a great affliction. If people could only believe it there were too many mourners in Northern homes for mirth and feasting to prevail.

There were some other redeeming points in this war. The excellence of the hospitals and the tender care for the wounded surpassed, as seems to be generally admitted, all previous efforts of humanity in that sad field, and the proportion of recoveries appears to have exceeded all experience. Here, again, we see besides the remarkable power of spontaneous organisation (for much of the work was done by voluntary effort), the regard paid by a democratic community to the meanest as well as the most important of its members. These soldiers were not mere food for the cannon. The women, too, appear to have done their part in this work of patriotism and humanity, and to have put away from themselves the reproach of having been flattered and pampered into frivolity and uselessness. It was something also that the inventive faculties of an industrial people should tell for so much in the production of new weapons and ships, of new military contrivances and constructions of all kinds; that intelligence should thus, even in war, have gained the mastery over brute force; and that means should have been prepared by which society may possibly one day annul the power of those drilled masses, which at present press so heavily on the liberties of the world.

In proportion as the struggle was for a moral object its effects upon the national character will be, and in some respects have been good. The nation has gained in dignity and self-respect. A just pride has cast out weak vanity, and abated the loud boastfulness which at first turned many hearts away from the Federal cause. The habit of swagger sensibly diminished as the stern struggle went on. Before, America had no history : her cravings for one were visible in the anxiety with which the most equivocal monuments of antiquity were preserved. Now she has a history which even the war powers of the Old World must respect and acknowledge as a title to the fellowship of great nations. True independence has been achieved, and the same slavish homage will no longer be paid, under the mask of ostentatious disdain, to the ideas and influences of the Old World. A manlier tone begins to pervade public and private life. Types of genuine worth have superseded empty demagogism in the allegiance of the national heart. The excess of the democratic spirit has been corrected by military discipline ; and the moral courage of rulers, and their firmness in the exercise of lawful authority, have increased. Patriotism has been stimulated so much, that a nationality too intense and narrow, too like that which incessant wars have engendered in European communities, is the thing at present to be feared. Soon the fruits of quickened intellect, as well as those of regenerated character may begin to appear. Soon we may see in America something like that burst of mental life which has followed and rewarded great moral struggles in the case of other nations : which followed and rewarded the struggle of Athens against the Persians : the struggle of Elizabethan England against Philip II. Already, indeed, the political intellect of the people has been elevated and ennobled by the practical discussion of the grandest questions on which political intellect can be engaged ; and of this high training there is more, perhaps there is only too much, yet to come.

Before the war America hardly possessed any grand examples of public character saving that of Washington, which was somewhat remote and somewhat aristocratic. The public men of the democracy lacked the potent teaching of such examples, and this was one cause of the want of dignity in American statesmen. A democratic leader scarcely knew what his ideal was. Now, new examples have been added of the true democratic type. The nation has been greater in this struggle than the individual men : but judged by the average standard of other nations and times, America in the civil war can scarcely be said to have been barren of great men. Two or three might be named who are still living. One has finished his course. In his perfect simplicity of character, as well as in his perfect devotion to the public good, Mr. Lincoln presented the ideal of a true servant of the people. The almost absolute ruler of a mighty nation, the chief of the greatest armaments in the world, he never allowed himself, in language or demeanour, to be exalted above his fellows, or to claim for himself the respect which was due to his place alone. No state surrounded his person. We have too good reason to know that this tyrant kept no guard. His example and the type of character which he has set before public men, as much as the victory which his patient wisdom, his constancy, and integrity mainly achieved, will protect for ever the cause for which he toiled and died ; so that, in his own words, government for the people and by the people shall never perish from the earth.

It would be wickedness, the greatest wickedness, to make a eulogy of war. War, besides the misery that it inflicts, stirs up from their depths all the evil passions of

F

human nature. If this conflict could be painted to the life, in all its details, the picture would no doubt teem, even on the Federal side, with things shocking and vile : with violence, rapine, depravity, and corruption. But it may truly be said that taken as a whole, and compared with other civil wars, it has displayed the growing ascendancy of influences which will at last banish all civil war, and all war, from the earth.

The power put forth by the American Commonwealth has secured another object most valuable to humanity. The Monroe doctrine, properly understood, and as Canning, who was really its first propounder, understood it, means not the aggrandisement of the United States, but the independence of America. It means that the Powers of the Past may work their will in their own Europe for a season ; but that they shall not be allowed to mar the hopes of man in the New World. The American Republic is not propagandist. Neither by violence nor by intrigue does it threaten any established government with subversion. Its citizens indeed are almost too regardless of the fate of the old nations, and too much inclined to treat freedom as a privilege of their own, not as the heritage of mankind. In this they are true to the example of their race which, in its revolutions, has always been content with asserting English rights. But they are warranted in defending, they are even bound to the extent of their power to defend, from the intrusion of propagandist despotism and aristocracy a hemisphere destined for other things. French Imperialism, which is as little capable of enduring the reproachful existence of freedom as Slavery was, took advantage of the distress of the American Republic to propagate itself, with its ecclesiastical and social appen-

dages, in Mexico. It may have cause to rue, perhaps it
already has cause to rue the hour.

To be just we must not forget to pay a tribute to the
valour of the Southerners, sullied as it was at Fort Pillow,
at Andersonville, and on other occasions, by the ferocity of
barbarians. In some of them this valour was inspired by
a love of independence and a sincere belief in State Rights
which mingled with and partly redeemed the more criminal
object for which they fought. It receives its reward,
not only in the respect which proved valour ensures, but
far more in liberation from the worst doom which can fall
on man, that of being the active minister of evil. To
oppress is worse than to be oppressed. If Slavery is
degradation to the slave, it is far deeper degradation to the
master; and emancipation is a far greater boon to the
master than to the slave. To that cruel, corrupt, and
barbarous society a hope of better things has come, though
in the stern form of conquest. A sea of blood has been
shed in this war, but on neither side has it been shed
entirely in vain.

The curtain has fallen upon the great drama of war.
It rises for a political drama equally great. The work of
reconstruction presents problems which will tax to the
utmost the practical sagacity of the American people; but
in that sagacity I have almost unbounded faith. It is the
quality not of isolated statesmen, with difficulty dragging
the dull masses after them, but of a whole nation, capable
of entering into political questions, and at once supporting
and correcting the action of the government, which is in
fact only the organ of the people. For ultimate reconciliation, when once the actual wound shall have been healed,
and the blackened relics of the war shall have disappeared,

the clemency of the conqueror has nobly paved the way ; and from the moment when I saw the temper of the Northern people I doubted as little of the possibility of restoring the Union as I did of Federal victory. The debt is a grave danger, rather from the political difficulties incident to the distribution of the burden than from its actual amount compared with the resources of the nation ; but prompt economy and a quick return to sound principles of finance have already restored the value of the national securities ; the people will always support as far as they can the credit of a government with which they are identified ; and, as in the case of Florence, so in the case of this great community of labour in America, the industry and frugality of a hive in which there are no drones will soon repair the waste of war. Protection indeed adds greatly to the gravity of the situation, political as well as financial, and threatens a new disruption of interests, as well as an increase of contrabandism dangerous to the character of the nation : but over this too, as I believe, the good sense of the mass of the people will prevail ; and it has been justly observed that in the case of America, the difficulty is not aggravated by the existence of a great territorial aristocracy, identified in interest with the Protectionist party. Nor does it appear that there is much reason in this case to apprehend the reaction which commonly ensues after violent revolutions. Political extravagance, such as the attempt of the French Revolutionists suddenly to grasp political perfection, is sure to be followed by a fatal collapse. But this has been a wise and sober, though terrible struggle, for the preservation of the State ; and therefore it does not seem likely to entail as its result the penalty that belongs to madness.

Some reaction after such enthusiasm—some relaxation of the sinews after such a tension, must be expected; but America is in no danger of sinking, like France, into political apathy and despair.

The most tremendous problem of all, is not the restoration of the Union, nor the discharge of fiscal liabilities, nor anything of a purely political kind; it is the re-organisation of society at the South. To this operation the eyes of all men may well be turned: it is perhaps the hardest ever undertaken by statesmen. Jamaica tells us with terrible emphasis what are the perils of a community composed of the ex-slave owner and the ex-slave. How can these perils be avoided? What will cleanse away the taint which seems not to quit the blood of the man who has owned slaves—or of his children—or of his children's children? How, with the ineradicable difference of colour, to which fatal memories will long cling, and with the physical antipathy the existence of which it is vain to deny, can we hope for social fusion? Without social fusion, how can we hope for political equality? And without political equality, what security can there be for justice? Kindness and wisdom would cure, in course of time, the slowly receding vices of the slave. Fair wages, paid at set of sun, so that even his shortened vision may see his reward as he works, would in time teach him industry: education, in the course of two or three generations, would raise his intelligence, and give him the power of self guidance. But the kindness and wisdom that might do this, in whom are they to be found? As to the theories about the incurable indolence and the incurable ferocity of the negro,—they will claim attention when a particle of historical evidence has been produced in their

support. As the case at present stands, the possibility of
curing the indolence and the ferocity of the whites at the
South is a much graver question. The negroes made good
soldiers when they were well commanded ; and when they
have been fairly tried they have made industrious work-
men. The late war, by putting their masters in many
places into their power, gave their ferocity full play; yet I
believe there was scarcely a single well-attested instance
of negro revenge. If the race had been really ferocious
they would not have been slaves ; to make the Red Indian
a slave would be no easy task. This figment of indelible
inferiority has been coined against oppressed nations as
well as against oppressed races ; ever since the days of the
ancient slave-owner, who held the fathers of great European nations in bondage as indelibly his inferiors, it has
been the well-known stock-in-trade of philosophic rapine.
It is not in the hopeless defects of the negro that the
difficulty lies ; it is in the relations between the master
and slave race when they are set to live together as fellow
citizens. And this is a problem of which (though perhaps
we may see the dawn of success in the changed position
which, partly in consequence of the exigencies of the war
itself, industry has assumed at the South, and in the pro-
bable influx of Northern employers at least into the Middle
States) we can only watch the solution with intense
sympathy and interest. Providence is inexhaustible ; and
in the New World many things are new. A way may yet
be found to form out of the two races, and by a combination of their different faculties and powers, a society,
different perhaps in its structure from Northern society,
yet equally based on justice.

If this had been a mere struggle for empire, it would

scarcely have lead to a corresponding conflict of parties in
this country. Being a struggle for great principles and
objects most vital to humanity, it did lead to such a conflict. And that conflict gave birth to the Society the
existence of which terminates to-day. We will not dwell
long on this part of our theme. Among the papers of Mr.
Lincoln was found, I am told, one which showed that he
intended, as a part of his policy of reconstruction, to destroy
all the trophies and monuments of the civil war. The parts
of men have for the most part been cast for them by ante-
cedent circumstances ; and all, except minds of remarkable
independence, must play their allotted part. That the
territorial aristocracy of this country and the clergy of the
Established Church should vehemently sympathise, even
with the Slave Power, against a community which though,
as I have said, not propagandist, was still the chief embodi-
ment and the hope of the principles most opposed to their
own, was natural; and we ought rather to dwell with
gratitude on the exceptions, than to blame those who obeyed
the prevailing impulse, and followed the general rule.
Although, could these friends of order and religion but
have seen it, all order, all religion, all conservatism even,
in the only rational and moral sense of the word, were
on the side of those who were defending against violence
the established constitution and the established principles of the United States. Conservatives must not think
that they can sanction violence till the law is settled
in their own favour, and thenceforth permit it no more.
They will find that violence, once let in, subverts all law,
and that the party which, in the long run, has most reason
to dread the inroads of physical force is that which, in the
long run, has not physical force upon its side. This is no

superfluous or irrelevant remark, when that strange and
fearful epilogue to the civil war in America, the Jamaica
Massacre, is about, apparently, to become the subject of a
party contest. Of course, though persons may be held
blameless for having played their natural parts, inferences
will be drawn from what has passed as to the character of
institutions. Men cannot be forbidden to ask whether a
nobility, which casts in its lot with slave-owners, is a
nobility indeed, really transcending in nobleness the na-
tures of ordinary men, so that the world still needs it,
and ought to make great sacrifices to maintain it as a type
of exalted humanity and a cynosure of honour, or whether
the day is not approaching when society must let chivalry
rest with the dust of the Crusaders, and take up with
homely justice. Men cannot be forbidden to ask whether
it is really well to let political power impose upon us
spiritual guides, when the guides it imposes have, in this
the most manifest conflict, as it seems to those who think
as we do, between Good and Evil which has been waged
in our days, almost unanimously taken the side of Evil;
when they have gone up into their pulpits to preach a
religion of purity and mercy, and come down from the
pulpit to stand side by side with atheist sciolism in defence
of Slavery and the Jamaica Massacre. Patient confidence
in progress and in the future of Humanity, not impatient
desire of sudden change, much less of revolution, is the
sentiment which this great victory ought to inspire; but
we have had an experience which will be remembered in
the day when great political issues are tried, and when the
nation wavers between its hopes of the future and its fear
of breaking with the consecrated institutions of the past.
The conduct of these classes, however, I repeat, was natural,

and would not have deserved or excused a bitter word, if they could only have said frankly that they desired the downfall of institutions opposed to their own, instead of talking about their sympathy for the weak, and their respect for national independence, and their anxiety for the triumph of Free Trade. Equally natural, perhaps, with the conduct of the territorial aristocracy, was that of our commercial aristocracy, who again, with some exceptions, for which the whole order will some day be grateful, ranged themselves on the side of the South. The relations between employer and employed are not yet happily settled; and till, by a better understanding of mutual interests, and the removal of faults on both sides, they are happily settled, a certain division of sympathies is sure to be seen. Perhaps there are other things to be said about a large number of those who have grown suddenly rich, and have not been trained to feel an interest in anything but the security and enjoyment of wealth, which it is not necessary, and would not be agreeable to say, but which if said, would partly account for their conduct in the struggle which is just past. Below all these classes, however, there was a mass of loose and ignorant opinion, which, partly by the skilful manipulation of the slave-owners, who evidently knew the secret of dealing with the press, and the adroit suggestion of a false theory at the critical moment—partly by ignorant prejudices and fancies about American aggressiveness, was turned to the wrong side. The truth is, political principle among ourselves was during those years rather at a low ebb. We were passing through a phase very analagous to that which I have described as existing in America under the ascendancy of Slavery, before the great rally of morality at the North. The causes of the phenomenon in both cases were

nearly the same. Here, as well as there, there was a great
and rapid increase of wealth; and here, as well as there,
there was a temporary decay of faith. We had gone in fact
so far in the backward path that now, as in the time of
Charles I., our reactionary politicians seem to think that
they can set their feet on the Great Charter, and our reactionary ecclesiastics that, with a few bells and a little incense,
and a word or two whispered into the ears of wealthy
devotees, they can undo the Reformation. We have shared
the moral decline of America, and we shall share her
regeneration. Already a change is felt, and the breeze of
morning begins faintly to blow over the long stagnant sea.

To stem this tide of sympathy with the slave-owner;
to do justice to the large classes, especially the working
classes, of this country, who were not represented by the
reactionary press; to prevent the moral weight of England,
perhaps even her sword—from being cast at a momentous
crisis of human destiny into the scale of Slavery; to save
the honour of our country from being sullied by a great
apostasy; to confirm the Government in neutrality, and see
that it was a real neutrality, not a neutrality of *Alabamas;*
to keep alive, if possible, the good feeling between the two
kindred nations, and avert the deadly rupture, deadly not
only to England and America but to the highest interests
of mankind, which the Southern party in Parliament and
the Press were labouring to bring on,—this Association
and its sister associations were formed. They were not
formed till support had been organised in this country for
the South, so that our action, like that of the party in
America with which we sympathised, was strictly defensive.
We did not make the civil war, nor did we instigate the
Americans to make it. Most of those who are here can

probably say with me that they looked upon its approach with horror. There are not a few perhaps in this room whom it threatened with ruin. But when it had commenced, we took part with what we believed to be the right, and strove to prevent England from taking part with what we believed to be the wrong. There is no blood on our heads : there might have been blood on the heads of our opponents if they had succeeded in involving England and America in war. Charges were brought against us of folly, blindness, fanaticism, which the event has answered, and with which we need concern ourselves no more. It has been shown that it is not unwise sometimes to back the moral forces even against the military probabilities ; and on the other hand, that the shallow cunning which can purvey for the prejudices of a club is apt to be at fault when the moral forces are on the scene. We may not be versed in the mysteries of diplomacy, but we were not bad diplomatists when we did our utmost to counteract the efforts of the powerful party here, which would have estranged from us for ever the heart of the American people. The main end we had in view was not commercial ; but I do not think we counselled English commerce ill, or that English commerce now believes that we counselled it ill, in dissuading it from sending out *Alabamas*. We had no doubt a primary regard, as surely every Christian and every rational and large-minded patriot must have a primary regard, for the general interests of humanity, in which those of each individual nation are bound up. But I hope and believe that we at the same time did, and I am sure that we wished and endeavoured to do, that which was best for the interest and for the honour of our country.

If the object of the Association has been in any measure

fulfilled, if it contributed in any measure towards averting the evils which it was formed to avert, every member of it will have cause to look back with thankfulness to his connection with it; and we have all reason to be grateful to our President and to others who at the critical moment organised us and directed our efforts, not without labour, not without sacrifices, not I fear without incurring some of the penalties which men incur by boldly separating from those around them on a question of principle ; for all which I trust the recollection of the good they have done and the evil they have prevented will make them full amends. And especially is the gratitude of all in this place, and of society at large, due to those who have shown by the course they have taken in this question, that the interests of the great employer are not really opposed, and that his sympathies ought not to be opposed, to those of the working man. That hour of Federal despair was a testing hour. It searched the convictions of all classes and of all men, and severed the counterfeit liberalism from the true.

In concluding let us return for a moment to a part of the subject as to which we have always hoped that, in spite of sinister appearances, there could be no real division of sentiment among the English people. There can surely be few Englishmen, few fellow-countrymen of Pitt and Wilberforce, to whom the Abolition of Slavery, however accomplished, is not in itself welcome. Here we may meet again, and rejoice again to meet, many from whom we have been divided on other grounds. Since the advent of Christianity itself, few more blessed announcements have been made to man than this, that Slavery is dead, dead in its only great stronghold, and therefore virtually dead everywhere and for ever; though the institution may still linger in Cuba, and though the tendency and the temper may remain and threaten revolt against humanity in Jamaica and elsewhere. It is not only that the chains of the negro have been struck off, that the negro race is redeemed from boundless and endless misery, from boundless and endless degradation. In the person of the negro, the respect for humanity has been restored—the principles of Christian and civilised society have been vindicated—the rights and the hopes of labour have been rescued from the powers which had conspired against them. It is a victory in which every man, high or low, who lives by the sweat of his brow has a part—in which every man who lives by the sweat of his brow has reason to rejoice. Be these the last words of the Association which ends its course to-night, SLAVERY IS DEAD EVERYWHERE AND FOR EVER.

REPORT OF THE FINAL MEETING

OF THE

UNION AND EMANCIPATION SOCIETY

(Published by desire of the Society).

At a General Meeting of the Union and Emancipation Society, held in the Town Hall, Manchester, January 22nd, 1866, THOMAS BAYLEY POTTER, Esq., M.P., President of the Society, in the chair, the following Report was read by Mr. E. O. GREENING, one of the Honorary Secretaries :—

REPORT

OF THE EXECUTIVE COMMITTEE TO THE MEMBERS AND FRIENDS OF THE UNION AND EMANCIPATION SOCIETY, AT THEIR LAST MEETING.

THE Executive of the Union and Emancipation Society, in presenting their final Report, congratulate the members and friends of the Association on the auspicious termination of their labours.

Five years ago a section of the United States of America, then known as the Slave States, sought by revolt and armed force the disruption of the Republic, and declared an intention to establish a Confederacy, whose corner stone should be Slavery.

To aid in the accomplishment of this gigantic crime societies were established in this country ; and the press, the platform, and the pulpit became to a very large extent sympathetic with the wicked enterprise. The aristocracy, the gentry, and the commercial classes (with many noble individual exceptions), were dragging the nation into a partisanship with rebellion and slavery.

At this critical period the Union and Emancipation Society was organised ; "to give expression, on behalf of "the population of this district, to their earnest sympathy "with the cause of Freedom, and fraternal regard towards "their kinsmen of the United States ; and to resist all "recognition of the Slaveholding Confederacy."

The inaugural address of the Society soon elicited an approving response, both in this country and in the colonies. Adhesions were enrolled of representative men, eminent in thought and action, from all parts of the kingdom, along with many thousands of the industrial classes.

The Executive disseminated, by means of the press and the platform, the most accurate information upon the political and social history of the United States ; the powers of the individual states ; the prerogatives of the Federal Government ; and particularly as to the causes and objects of the Rebellion.

It was soon demonstrated that the *people* were emphatically true to their ancient love of freedom and constitutional government, and that the heart of England was sound on this great question.

Although the contest here, against the manifold agencies of the Slave Power, was severe and varying, ultimately the conscience and common sense of the people triumphed, in and out of Parliament, and the public mind became steadfast in favour of the policy of neutrality and non-recognition, and confirmed in the belief that slavery was doomed.

The progress of the conflict on the other side of the Atlantic, between the friends and foes of human liberty was watched by the Executive with deepening interest, but with unwavering confidence in the final triumph of freedom and civilisation.

Early in the year 1865, came the collapse and down-fall of the Slaveholders' Confederacy.

In the first year of peace, ere the nation had ceased to mourn the loss of thousands of her bravest sons, and the death of her Martyr-President, Abraham Lincoln, the people of the United States amended the Federal Constitution—abolishing and for ever prohibiting Slavery throughout their great Republic.

By this act millions of our fellow creatures emerged from the condition of chattlehood into the higher region of manhood ; the stain which had disfigured the national flag of the United States was removed ; all her fruitful lands were opened to the civilising and ennobling influ-ences of free labour ; and the blessings of free schools, a free press, and free government were secured as an inheritance for ever.

The United States have thus proved to the world that " a government of the people, by the people, for the people," is competent to organise and wield vast combina-tions of power ; to administer resources of extraordinary magnitude ; to carry out the highest purposes of states-manship to their most successful issues ; and in the hour of triumph can exhibit a moderation of spirit and clemency towards the vanquished unexampled in history.

The spectacle of hundreds of thousands of patriot soldiers returning to their peaceful callings and the duties of citizenship, is another suggestive lesson to the unen-franchised peoples, taxed to support the military mo-narchies of Europe.

We commend to the benevolent consideration of our countrymen the claims of the freedmen of the United States, whose sufferings, in their transition from bondage

G

to liberty, appeal to the generous instincts of our common humanity. We also especially urge the claims of the still-oppressed freed people in some of our own colonies, for the wellbeing of whom we are more directly responsible; and whose wretched condition calls for a practical manifestation of our Christian sympathy.

In conclusion, we offer our congratulations to our transatlantic friends, on the restoration of peace, the preservation of the Union, and the emancipation of the slave; and whilst not unmindful of the difficulties that surround their President, we recognise his patriotism, moral courage, and practical statesmanship, and record our earnest hope that in the discharge of the functions of his high office, he will secure beyond compromise all the rights and privileges of citizenship to his countrymen, without distinction of colour.

APPENDIX TO THE REPORT.

PROCEEDINGS IN REFERENCE TO THE ASSASSINATION OF PRESIDENT LINCOLN.

At a meeting held in the Free Trade Hall, Manchester, April 28th, 1865,

FRANCIS TAYLOR, Esq., in the chair :

It was moved by the Rev. G. W. CONDER, seconded by JACOB BRIGHT, Esq., and passed unanimously :—

"That the address of sympathy and condolence with Mrs. Lincoln, now read, be adopted, and that the

Chairman be authorised to sign it on behalf of this meeting."

" *To Mrs. Lincoln.*

"MADAM,—It is not for us to invade the privacy of domestic sorrow, nor fitting that we should add to the sharpness of your grief by characterising as it deserves the deed which has deprived you of a husband and your country of its chief magistrate. We desire, however, to express our deep sympathy with you in this mournful affliction, and our earnest hope that you may be supported through the trial by the consciousness that your husband, though called to the helm in the midst of tempest and storm, never failed to respond to the call of duty, and that throughout a period of unparalleled difficulty he has guided the affairs of the nation in a manner which will ever connect his name with all that is noble, magnanimous, and great in your country's history. His name will be associated with the cause of human freedom throughout all time ; and generations yet unborn will learn to lisp his name as synonymous with Liberty itself, and to connect the atrocious deed by which his career was closed with the expiring throes of that foul system of Slavery against which his life was a standing protest, and the fate of which he had sealed.

" For and on behalf of the Union and Emancipation Society,

" THOMAS BAYLEY POTTER, President.

" FRANCIS TAYLOR (for self and other Vice-Presidents).

" SAMUEL WATTS, Treasurer.

" J. H. ESTCOURT (Chairman of the Executive Com-

" J. C. EDWARDS, } Honorary Secretaries. [mittee.)
" E. O. GREENING, }

" 51, Piccadilly, Manchester, 27th April, 1865."

Moved by Alderman HEYWOOD, seconded by the Rev.
S. A. STEINTHAL, supported by J. BERRY TORR, Esq.:

> "That the address to President Johnson, expressive of
> sympathy with the American people in the loss
> they have sustained by the lamented death of
> President Lincoln, be adopted, and that the Chair-
> man be authorised to sign it on behalf of this
> meeting."

"*To His Excellency Andrew Johnson, President of the
United States.*

"SIR,—We have heard with profound regret that your
late distinguished President, Abraham Lincoln, has fallen
a victim to a vile conspiracy, and that he has been suddenly removed from your midst by the hands of a cowardly
assassin.

"We have watched his career from the period of his
election, in 1860, down to his lamented death, as well
through all the darkest hours of the struggle in which
your country has been engaged, as at the time when success seemed to be within his grasp, and we have ever
recognised in him a self-denying patriotism, a devotion to
the principles of right and justice, and a determination to
surmount, by constitutional means, every obstacle which
stood in the way of the final triumph of those principles.
His unswerving faith never forsook him in the hour of
depression and gloom, and he has left behind him a noble
example of magnanimity and moderation in the hour of
victory, which cannot fail to secure the admiration of the
whole civilised world.

"Elected on the basis of a limitation of the area of

Slavery in the United States, he gradually and cautiously developed an Anti-Slavery policy, which resulted in the issue of an Emancipation Proclamation, by which every slave in the rebel States is now free; and he lived to see adopted by Congress an amendment of the constitution abolishing for ever Slavery in the United States.

" He has not been permitted to witness the final achievement of this great work, but his name will ever be associated in history with the removal of this dark stain from your national escutcheon.

" It is not alone, or chiefly on grounds of philanthropy that we have sympathised in his objects and aims. From the period when we beheld a section of your community, when defeated at the ballot box, appealing to the arbitrament of the sword, without even the pretence of a grievance, excepting the alleged danger to the institution of Slavery, we regarded free constitutional government as on its trial, and we have viewed with unvarying satisfaction the uniform consistency with which he always upheld the maintenance of the Union as paramount to every other consideration.

" In the recollection of these things, we desire now, through you, to express our deep sympathy with your loyal fellow-citizens in the grievous loss you have sustained: a loss which, at this important crisis in your country's history, cannot fail to produce serious and anxious concern.

" In the midst of gloom, however, we are consoled by the reflection that the world is ruled by principles—not by men; and that while the most distinguished statesmen are constantly passing away, the principles which they have propounded are immortal.

" Mr. Lincoln, it is true, has departed, but he has bequeathed to posterity an example which cannot fail to exercise a powerful influence on the future of your country.

"The constitution places you in the office of Chief Magistrate of the Union at a solemn crisis in your national affairs, which has no parallel in past history ; but we cheerfully recognise the fact that the same ballot which secured the triumphant re-election of Mr. Lincoln, also placed you in the distinguished position to become his successor ; and our faith in the instincts of a great people forbids us to doubt that the noble principles which animated him will ever find a response in your heart.

　　"For and on behalf of the Union and Emancipation
　　　　Society,
　　　　　　"THOMAS BAYLEY POTTER, President.
　　　　　　"FRANCIS TAYLOR (for self and other
　　　　　　　　Vice-Presidents).
　　　　　　"SAML. WATTS, Treasurer.
　　　　　　"J. H. ESTCOURT, Chairman of Executive.
　　　　　　"J. C. EDWARDS, ⎫
　　　　　　"E. O. GREENING, ⎬Hon. Secretaries.
　　"51, Piccadilly, Manchester, 27th April, 1865."

It was further resolved :—

　　"That this meeting also desires to record an expression
　　of profound sympathy with the Honourable W. H.
　　Seward and the members of his family, in regard
　　to the atrocious attempt to assassinate that distin-
　　guished and able statesman whilst lying in a help-
　　less condition on a bed of sickness; and this meeting
　　earnestly hopes that the foul attempt may not have
　　proved successful, but that Mr. Seward may soon be
　　restored to health and vigour to render efficient

service in the government of his great nation, under a restored Union, based on the eternal principle of freedom, justice, and equal rights to men of all races."

FRANCIS TAYLOR,
Chairman.

———

" Department of State,
" Washington, May 16, 1865.

" SIR,—I have the honour to acknowledge with very sincere pleasure the receipt of your letter of the 28th ultimo, enclosing a copy of a resolution passed unanimously at a crowded meeting of the citizens of Manchester, held in the Free Trade Hall, relative to the late tragic occurrences in this capital.

" The sympathy so kindly and cordially expressed in this resolution will be gratefully appreciated by Mr. Seward, who, I am happy to state, is fast recovering from his injuries, as well as by the various members of his family.

" I am, Sir, very respectfully,
" Your obedient Servant,
" W. HUNTER, Acting Secretary.
" To Mr. Francis Taylor, Manchester, England."

———

" Department of State,
" Washington, 11th November, 1865.

" To the Union and Emancipation Society of Manchester.

" GENTLEMEN,—I am directed by the President of the United States to return to you his very sincere acknowledgments and thanks for the liberal and kind address which you made to him on his accession to the Chief Magistracy in April last.

"It would be doing you a great injustice, however, to confine this acknowledgment to that address. Your enlightened, truthful, faithful advocacy of the cause of the American Republic and of humanity during the agitations of the past four years entitles your Society to an honourable place in American history, and the history of our age.

"It is a matter of constant regret on my part that, owing to a temporary derangement of business in this Department, which has existed during a portion of the year, the President's directions in regard to this acknowledgment, and many others, justly due to the friends of our country abroad, as well as at home, have been performed dilatorily and imperfectly.

"I have the honour to inform you that your affecting address to Mrs. Mary Lincoln (which was received by me at the same time with your address to the President) was, without delay, placed in her hands.

"I have the honour to be, Gentlemen,
"Your obedient Servant,
"WILLIAM H. SEWARD."

Note.—Your Committee have issued and circulated upwards of *four hundred thousand* books, pamphlets, and tracts, during the three years of its operations ; and nearly *five hundred* official and public meetings have been held in the promotion of the objects of the Society.

MANCHESTER,
22nd January, 1866.

Moved by FRANCIS TAYLOR, Esq., seconded by SAMUEL WATTS, Esq., and unanimously adopted :

"That the Report now read be adopted ; and that the thanks of the Union and Emancipation Society are now specially presented to the Executive Committee for their administration of the affairs of the society."

Professor GOLDWIN SMITH then delivered an address on the "Civil War in America."

Moved by GEO. SHAW LEFEVRE, Esq., M.P., seconded by Dr. SANDWITH, C.B. (of Kars):

"That the thanks of this meeting be given to Professor Goldwin Smith for his able and interesting address on the 'Civil War in America,' and that he be requested to allow the address to be published."

Moved by J. H. ESTCOURT, Esq., seconded by Dr. J. WATTS:

"That the following Address to the President be adopted:—

"*Address presented to Thomas Bayley Potter, M.P., President of the Union and Emancipation Society of Manchester, at a Special General Council, held on the 22nd January, 1866.*

"SIR,—The Executive and Members of the Union and Emancipation Society, in General Council assembled, present this expression of their grateful appreciation of the valuable services rendered by you as its President.

"When the friends of Freedom and good government in this country were too generally silent and inactive in regard to the Slaveholders' Rebellion in the Southern States of America, you boldly allied yourself with the working men in forming this Association, which proclaimed as its cardinal points the maintenance of the Federal Union, and the Abolition of Negro Slavery in the United States.

" This movement, by embracing both the political and philanthropic elements of that great struggle, was in advance of the action of the then existing organisations, and events have shown that it was more in consonance with the spirit and necessities of the crisis.

" Sympathisers with the Slave Power had already established societies to excite the passions and mould the opinions of the people into an approval of the so-called Confederacy; but the labours of this society demonstrated to our American brethren that the majority of the people were as true as ever in their admiration of free institutions, and their hatred to Slavery.

" The General Council, at this, their last meeting, sincerely thank you for the munificent aid you have so cheerfully given to sustain their operations, and to accomplish the objects of the Society ; and they trust that you may long live to continue your patriotic labours in the cause of progress, and to realise your earnest aspirations for the political enfranchisement of all nations."

The following names are attached to the Address :—

Vice-Presidents.

Thomas Bazley, Esq., M.P.

E. A. Leatham, Esq.

P. A. Taylor, Esq., M.P.

Guildford J. H. Onslow, Esq., M.P., Winchester.

Thomas Hughes, Esq., M.P.

Duncan M'Laren, M.P., Edinburgh.

John Stuart Mill, Esq., M.P., London.

Lieut.-General T. Perronet Thompson.

Professor J. E. Cairns, A.M., Dublin.
Professor Jno. Nichol, Glasgow.
Professor Goldwin Smith, Oxford.
Professor F. W. Newman, London.
Professor Beesly, London.
Professor J. E. Thorold Rogers, Oxford.
Professor Rolleston, Oxford.
Professor Henry J. Stephen Smith, Oxford.
Professor Fawcett, Cambridge.
Professor Rogers, Glasgow.
Professor N. M'Michael, D.D., Dunfermline.
Hon. and Rev. Baptist W. Noel, London.
Rev. Leslie Stephen, Fellow of Trinity Hall, Cam-
Rev. Thomas Guthrie, D.D., Edinburgh.   [bridge.
Rev. Newman Hall, LL.B., London.
Rev. James W. Massie, D.D., LL.D., London.
Rev. Henry W. Crosskey, Glasgow.
Rev. Samuel Davidson, LL.D., London
Rev. Francis Bishop, Chesterfield.
Rev. J. Parker, D.D., Manchester.
Rev. J. Robberds, B.A., Liverpool.
Rev. Marmaduke Miller, Darlington.
Rev. T. G. Lee, Salford.
Rev. Goodwyn Barmby, Wakefield.
Rev. C. M. Birrell, Liverpool.
Rev. Robert R. Drummond, B.A., Edinburgh.
Rev. Geo. Douglas Macgregor, Farnworth.
Rev. John Guttridge, Ex-President Methodist Free
Rev. Henry Batchelor, Glasgow.   [Church.
Rev. Henry Solly, London.
Rev. Robert Spears, London.
Rev. Edmond Kell, M.A., F.S.A., Southampton.

Rev. G. T. Fox, Durham.
W. Coningham, Esq., Brighton.
Charles Sturge, Esq., Birmingham.
G. L. Ashworth, Esq., Rochdale.
F. G. Haviland, Esq., Cambridge.
W. E. Adams, Esq., Newcastle-upon-Tyne.
W. P. Paton, Esq., Glasgow.
George Wilson, Esq., Manchester.
Dr. John Watts, Manchester.
Mr. Edward Hooson, Manchester.
Alderman Abel Heywood, Manchester.
Alderman Henry Brown, Bradford.
Alderman William Harvey, J.P., Salford.
Alderman Joseph H. Moore, Rochdale.
Councillor Murray, Manchester.
Councillor T. Warburton, Manchester.
Councillor George Booth, Manchester.
Councillor Clegg, Manchester.
Councillor Butterworth, Manchester.
Councillor Ogden, Manchester.
Councillor Ryder, Manchester.
Councillor J. R. Jeffery, Liverpool.
Councillor Hampson, Manchester.
W. J. Williams, Esq., Salford.
Max Kyllman, Esq., Manchester.
S. P. Robinson, Esq., Manchester.
H. M. Steinthal, Esq., Manchester.
Francis Taylor, Esq., Manchester.
Thomas Thomasson, Esq., Bolton.
Joseph Leese, Esq., Bowdon.
John Epps, Esq., M.D., London.
J. A. Langford, Esq., Birmingham.

J. J. Colman, Esq., Norwich.
James M'Clelland, Esq., Glasgow.
William Brown, Esq., Glasgow.
Edward Alexander, jun., Esq., Glasgow.
Councillor John Burt, Glasgow.
Charles Robertson, Esq., Glasgow.
Henry Lightbown, Esq., Pendleton.
Abraham Howarth, Esq., Manchester.
James M. Paton, Esq., Montrose.
Thos. R. Arnott, Esq., Liverpool.
E. K. Muspratt, Esq., Liverpool.
J. B. Whitehead, Esq., Rawtenstall.
Isaac B. Cooke, Esq., Liverpool.
Thomas Crosfield, Esq., Liverpool.
Robertson Gladstone, Esq., Liverpool.
John Patterson, Esq., Liverpool.
C. E. Rawlins, jun., Esq., Liverpool.
Robert Trimble, Esq., Liverpool.
Charles Wilson, Esq., Liverpool.
William Shaen, Esq., London.
Handel Cossham, Esq., Bristol.
Robert Kell, Esq., Bradford.
S. C. Kell, Esq., Bradford.
Richard C. Rawlings, Esq., Ruabon.
J. S. Barratt, Esq., Southport.
Thomas C. Riley, Esq., Wigan.
R. S. Ashton, Esq., Darwen.
Eccles Shorrock, Esq., Darwen.
John Crosfield, Esq., Warrington.
Jacob Bright, Esq.. Alderley.
John Petrie, Esq., Rochdale.
Oliver Ormerod, Esq., Rochdale.

J. C. Dyer, Esq., Burnage.

George Crosfield, Esq., Lymm.

F. Pennington, Esq., Alderley.

J. B. Forster, Esq., Manchester.

James Galloway, Esq., Manchester.

Charles Cheetham, Esq., Heywood.

Samuel Pope, Esq., Barrister-at-law.

Ernest Jones, Esq., Barrister-at-law.

Dr. Louis Borchardt, Manchester.

Charles H. Bracebridge, Esq.. Atherstone Hall.

William Jeffery Etches, Esq., Derby.

Mr. Serjeant Parry, London.

William Biggs, Esq., Leicester.

Andrew Leighton, Esq., Liverpool.

Edward Dicey, Esq., London.

James Ross, Esq., Carlisle.

Robert Ferguson, Esq., Carlisle.

Richard Johnson, Esq., Manchester.

Joseph Spencer, Esq., Manchester.

Thomas Spence, Esq., Barrister-at-law.

Arthur Trevelyan, Esq., J.P., Teinholm.

James M'Culloch, Esq., M D., Dumfries.

Peter Retford Scott, Esq., Edinburgh.

W. E. Hodgkinson, Esq., Manchester.

Sir John Hesketh Lethbridge, Bart., Taunton.

J. Mackenzie, Esq., M.D., J.P., Inverness.

Thomas Nelson, Esq., Edinburgh.

John Ashworth, Esq., J.P., Turton, near Bolton.

Thomas Emmott, Esq., Oldham.

William C. Leng, Esq., Sheffield.

Robert Service, Esq., Glasgow.

E. W. Thomas, Esq., Oswestry.

James Aytoun, Esq., London.

Hon. George Brown, Toronto.

Dr. Alexander, Edinburgh.

R. Peek, Esq., J.P., Hazlewood.

Colonel Henry Salwey, Runnymede Park, Egham.

James Taylor, jun., Esq., Birmingham.   [Oxford.

Charles Henry Robarts, Esq., B.A., Christ Church,

F. J. Furnivall, Esq., Barrister-at-Law, London.

E. Herbert Grundy, Esq., Manchester.

Frederick Harrison, Esq., Barrister-at-Law, London.

James Cropper, Esq., Kendal.

Thomas H. Bastard, Esq., Charlton, Blandford.

Samuel A. Goddard, Esq., Birmingham.

E. F. Flower, Esq., Stratford-on-Avon.

Robert Hyde Buckley, Esq., Mossley.

Samuel Watts, Esq., Manchester, *Treasurer.*

John H. Estcourt, Esq., *Chairman of Executive.*

John C. Edwards, } *Hon. Secretaries.*
Edward Owen Greening, }

Moved by the PRESIDENT, seconded by Mr. Councillor
MURRAY:

"That the sincere and earnest thanks of the Union
and Emancipation Society be given to Samuel
Watts, Treasurer; John Hart Estcourt, Chairman;
John C. Edwards, and Edward Owen Greening,
Honorary Secretaries, for their able and most inde-
fatigable services as officers of the Association."

The society was then formally dissolved.

THOMAS B. POTTER, Chairman.

The President having vacated the chair, it was taken by JOHN STUART, Esq.

Moved by Mr. Councillor RUMNEY, seconded by T. R. WILKINSON, Esq., supported by Mr. Alderman HEYWOOD, and unanimously adopted :

"That the thanks of the meeting be given to Mr. Thomas Bayley Potter, for his conduct in the chair."

JOHN STUART, Chairman.

www.ingramcontent.com/pod-product-compliance
Lightning Source LLC
Chambersburg PA
CBHW032358280326
41935CB00008B/624